Wim Wenders's Road Movie Philosophy

Philosophies of Education in Art, Cinema and Literature

Series Editors: René V. Arcilla and Megan J. Laverty

Books in the series examine the nature of formative education articulated in works of art, cinema, and literature. This series is motivated by the basic fact that we are all fated to age and grow up. Responding to what happens to us, we each give form to ourselves through memory, understanding, and narrative. Although the social sciences currently dominate our inquiry into this process, there are features of it that are better suited for philosophical study. Indeed, such an examination of the conceptual link between formation and education promises to have practical implications for how we engage in parenting, teaching, coaching, mentoring, and caregiving. Now the arts offer us a rich archive of depictions of how one becomes who one is. Our series will engage philosophically with such artworks with a view to deepening and complicating our understanding of this crucial humanizing process.

Editorial Board

Lawrence Blum, University of Massachusetts, Boston, USA
Ann Chinnery, Simon Fraser University, Canada
Christopher Cordner, University of Melbourne, Australia
Alice Crary, New School for Social Research, USA, and Oxford University, UK
Cora Diamond, University of Virginia, USA
Raimond Gaita, University of Melbourne, Australia
David T. Hansen, Teachers College, Columbia University, USA
Duck-Joo Kwak, Seoul National University, South Korea
Peter Roberts, University of Canterbury, New Zealand
Anna Pagès Santacana, Ramon Llull University, Spain
Paul Standish, University College London, UK
Craig Taylor, Flinders University, Australia

Wim Wenders's Road Movie Philosophy

Education Without Learning

René V. Arcilla

BLOOMSBURY ACADEMIC
LONDON • NEW YORK • OXFORD • NEW DELHI • SYDNEY

BLOOMSBURY ACADEMIC
Bloomsbury Publishing Plc
50 Bedford Square, London, WC1B 3DP, UK
1385 Broadway, New York, NY 10018, USA
29 Earlsfort Terrace, Dublin 2, Ireland

BLOOMSBURY, BLOOMSBURY ACADEMIC and the Diana logo
are trademarks of Bloomsbury Publishing Plc

First published in Great Britain 2020
Paperback edition first published 2021

Copyright © René V. Arcilla, 2020

René V. Arcilla has asserted his right under the Copyright,
Designs and Patents Act, 1988, to be identified as Author of this work.

Series design by Adriana Brioso
Cover image: Wim Wenders in Cannes, France, 1987. (© CHRISTOPHE D YVOIRE/
Sygma via Getty Images)

All rights reserved. No part of this publication may be reproduced or
transmitted in any form or by any means, electronic or mechanical,
including photocopying, recording, or any information storage or retrieval
system, without prior permission in writing from the publishers.

Bloomsbury Publishing Plc does not have any control over, or responsibility for,
any third-party websites referred to or in this book. All internet addresses given
in this book were correct at the time of going to press. The author and publisher
regret any inconvenience caused if addresses have changed or sites have
ceased to exist, but can accept no responsibility for any such changes.

A catalogue record for this book is available from the British Library.

A catalog record for this book is available from the Library of Congress.

ISBN: HB: 978-1-3501-1042-7
PB: 978-1-3502-1380-7
ePDF: 978-1-3501-1043-4
eBook: 978-1-3501-1044-1

Typeset by Deanta Global Publishing Services, Chennai, India

To find out more about our authors and books visit
www.bloomsbury.com and sign up for our newsletters.

To Gregg, Mark, Steve, and Achim

Contents

List of Illustrations		viii
Preface		xi
Introduction		1
1	*Alice in the Cities*	19
2	Related Road Movies	41
3	Genre Contrasts	71
4	Education Movies	103
5	Learning without Education	131
6	Coda	149
Index		155

Illustrations

1.1 *Alice in the Cities* directed by Wim Wenders © Filmverlag der Autoren, Munich/Westdeutscher Rundfunk, Cologne 1974. All rights reserved. 20
1.2 *Alice in the Cities* directed by Wim Wenders © Filmverlag der Autoren, Munich/Westdeutscher Rundfunk, Cologne 1974. All rights reserved. 21
1.3 *Alice in the Cities* directed by Wim Wenders © Filmverlag der Autoren, Munich/Westdeutscher Rundfunk, Cologne 1974. All rights reserved. 27
1.4 *Alice in the Cities* directed by Wim Wenders © Filmverlag der Autoren, Munich/Westdeutscher Rundfunk, Cologne 1974. All rights reserved. 31
1.5 *Alice in the Cities* directed by Wim Wenders © Filmverlag der Autoren, Munich/Westdeutscher Rundfunk, Cologne 1974. All rights reserved. 33
1.6 *Alice in the Cities* directed by Wim Wenders © Filmverlag der Autoren, Munich/Westdeutscher Rundfunk, Cologne 1974. All rights reserved. 38
2.1 *Kings of the Road* directed by Wim Wenders © Wim Wenders Produktion, Munich 1976. All rights reserved. 44
2.2 *Kings of the Road* directed by Wim Wenders © Wim Wenders Produktion, Munich 1976. All rights reserved. 47
2.3 *Paris, Texas* directed by Wim Wenders © Road Movies Filmproduktion, Berlin/Argos Film, Paris 1984. All rights reserved. 48
2.4 *Paris, Texas* directed by Wim Wenders © Road Movies Filmproduktion, Berlin/Argos Film, Paris 1984. All rights reserved. 53

2.5	*Until the End of the World* directed by Wim Wenders © Road Movies Filmproduktion, Berlin/Argos Film, Paris/Village Roadshow Pictures 1991. All rights reserved.	58
2.6	*Until the End of the World* directed by Wim Wenders © Road Movies Filmproduktion, Berlin/Argos Film, Paris/Village Roadshow Pictures 1991. All rights reserved.	59
2.7	*Land of Plenty* directed by Wim Wenders © Reverse Angle/IFC Films/InDigEnt 2004. All rights reserved.	64
2.8	*Don't Come Knocking* directed by Wim Wenders © Reverse Angle/Arte France Cinéma 2005. All rights reserved.	65
2.9	*Don't Come Knocking* directed by Wim Wenders © Reverse Angle/Arte France Cinéma 2005. All rights reserved.	67
3.1	*Land of Plenty* directed by Wim Wenders © Reverse Angle/IFC Films/InDigEnt 2004. All rights reserved.	81
3.2	*Lisbon Story* directed by Wim Wenders © Road Movies Filmproduktion, Berlin 1994. All rights reserved.	84
3.3	*Tokyo-ga* directed by Wim Wenders © Road Movies Filmproduktion, Berlin/Chris Sievernich Produktion, Berlin/Gray City Inc. 1985. All rights reserved.	87
3.4	*Tokyo-ga* directed by Wim Wenders © Road Movies Filmproduktion, Berlin/Chris Sievernich Produktion, Berlin/Gray City Inc. 1985. All rights reserved.	87
3.5	*The American Friend* directed by Wim Wenders © Road Movies Filmproduktion, Berlin/Wim Wenders Produktion, Munich/Les Films du Losange, Paris/Westdeutscher Rundfunk, Cologne 1977. All rights reserved.	93
3.6	*The American Friend* directed by Wim Wenders © Road Movies Filmproduktion, Berlin/Wim Wenders Produktion, Munich/Les Films du Losange, Paris/Westdeutscher Rundfunk, Cologne 1977. All rights reserved.	94
3.7	*Wrong Move* directed by Wim Wenders © Solaris Film, Munich/Westdeutscher Rundfunk, Cologne 1975. All rights reserved.	97
3.8	*Wrong Move* directed by Wim Wenders © Solaris Film, Munich/Westdeutscher Rundfunk, Cologne 1975. All rights reserved.	100

4.1 *Wings of Desire* directed by Wim Wenders © Road Movies Filmproduktion, Berlin/Argos Films, Paris/Westdeutscher Rundfunk, Cologne 1987. All rights reserved. 105

4.2 *Wings of Desire* directed by Wim Wenders © Road Movies Filmproduktion, Berlin/Argos Films, Paris/Westdeutscher Rundfunk, Cologne 1987. All rights reserved. 109

4.3 *Palermo Shooting* directed by Wim Wenders © Neue Road Movies/Arte France Cinéma/Zweites Deutsches Fernsehen 2008. All rights reserved. 112

4.4 *Palermo Shooting* directed by Wim Wenders © Neue Road Movies/Arte France Cinéma/Zweites Deutsches Fernsehen 2008. All rights reserved. 115

4.5 *The Salt of the Earth* directed by Wim Wenders © Decia Films/Amazonas Images/Solares Fondazione delle Arti 2014. All rights reserved. 119

4.6 *The Salt of the Earth* directed by Wim Wenders © Decia Films/Amazonas Images/Solares Fondazione delle Arti 2014. All rights reserved. 120

4.7 *Every Thing Will Be Fine* directed by Wim Wenders © Neue Road Movies/Montauk Productions/BAC Films Production/Göta Film/MER Film 2015. All rights reserved. 124

4.8 *Every Thing Will Be Fine* directed by Wim Wenders © Neue Road Movies/Montauk Productions/BAC Films Production/Göta Film/MER Film 2015. All rights reserved. 126

Preface

It was in the mid-1970s, while I was in college, when I saw my first work of Wim Wenders. A campus society, Doc Films, organized a screening of *Kings of the Road* (1976). Even after having watched that movie innumerable times afterward, I can still remember how initially impressed I was by its countercultural ethos. Its tone of day-to-day, small adventures, gentle humor, melancholy, and wandering restlessness captured precisely what it felt like to me to live one's youth in the ebbing of the hopes of the sixties. The film's sad yet principled renunciation of forcefulness seemed natural and utterly convincing. My friends and I recognized a kinship with its director and we made it a point to catch his films whenever we could.

As the years since that viewing have stretched into decades, the sense that Wenders is chronicling the end of '60s youth has inevitably faded. His succeeding films express little interest in nostalgia; they are resolutely responsive to the changing dramas of their times. While I continue to find something consistently winning about this work, I too have no interest in dwelling on the past. Until recently, I had barely thought about the impact that his pictures had on me at the start.

This changed when I found myself one day mulling over a dean's response to a course proposal of mine for our school. He was generally supportive of my new, liberal-arts offering designed for a general audience, but he warned me against using in the title the word *education*. "That will be an immediate turn-off for most students." I knew what he meant, of course. A course about education sounds like it is addressed mainly to would-be school teachers and administrators, or to researchers of these professions and of schooling. The sort of people who are attracted to grand questions like those of justice or nihilism are apt to dismiss the topic of education as too specialized, dry, and occupational.

The more I thought about this, though, the more uncanny this understanding appeared. Why exactly do we look at education in this way? It would be as if whenever someone invoked the question of nihilism, we immediately thought of competing psychological treatments for depression, or whenever someone drew attention to the political dimension of life, we immediately weighed things in terms of legislative tactics. Surely, there is likewise something more at stake in *education* than access, efficiency, and accountability, and selection protocols, school budgets, and added value? When we consider the full meaning of the word, is it not one that should also evoke a whole dimension of the human drama?

These reflections led me to realize that what I want to study is education outside of schooling. A couple of additional memories helped crystalize this project for me. The first concerns a moment in college when a friend of mine abruptly dropped out. Despite doing well in classes and being one of the most intellectual people I knew, she declared that she wanted to go looking in the world for a real education. Interestingly, I knew exactly what she meant. Indeed, her idea did not seem especially peculiar or original at the time; lots of people my age then shared that longing, even if, like me, they lacked the courage to act on it. Education unsheltered, exposed to the world, was in the air in my youth. And it was portrayed in an especially perceptive and moving way, I then recalled, in Wenders's road movies.

What is the nature of our education in the wild? How are we each drawn into its drama and what are some of the diverse, yet recognizable, ways that we can live this drama satisfyingly? Indeed, in this education, how could our very destinies be at stake? These are the questions this book addresses. As I shall explain, they are both compellingly raised and insightfully responded to by Wenders's road movie oeuvre. My study of it thus amounts to an argument for why and how its works, and others like them, can contribute to an appreciation that nothing educational, in the profoundest sense, is foreign to us.

* * *

Many people have contributed vitally to this writing project. Thinking of them brings joy and fills me with gratitude.

My parents, siblings, and in-laws were an inexhaustible source of encouragement and support. Their wind at my back gave each advance an air of inevitability.

Friend after friend took pains to sit down with me to discuss my ideas; some of them read portions of the manuscript in draft and volunteered detailed comments. Rather than distinguish them by name, I trust they know who they are and how much I appreciate their camaraderie. Patiently and generously, these interlocutors made my questions their own and thought through them together with me. My work is better for all their criticism and advice.

At Bloomsbury, my commissioning editor, Mark Richardson, believed in this book from the start and has never tired of reaffirming its meaning to me. He has also been a solid source of guidance in the preparation of the manuscript. Megan Laverty, my book series coeditor, scrutinized the last draft as a whole and gave me a number of key, constructive suggestions.

Finally, my deepest thanks go to my closest collaborator, Patricia. In so many, quite literal ways, she has lived virtually every sentence with me. Every time I needed to consider the divergent directions opening up to be understood in the text, she was there. From her, I am educated anew each day that thinking is conversational.

This book is dedicated to my old *Wanderjahrgefährten*, in celebration of our ongoing journey in friendship.

Introduction

Imagine that we suddenly encounter outer space aliens. Once the shock and fear has abated, let us suppose that, eventually, enough communication and trust is established between the two species that each is invited to send to the other planet a team of anthropologists (or the alien equivalent). After our scientists have been away for a while, they begin to send back some disturbing reports. The aliens, it appears, utterly lack the concept of romantic love. There is, to be sure, plenty of sexual activity, which their culture celebrates as a source of pleasure, health, and comic intrigue. The children that are the fruit of some of this activity receive the same care as our own, only from a quasi-family which includes, but is not centered on, the birth parents, as in a radical commune. Associated with sex, then, is salubrious fun and a share in the responsibility of raising the next generation. Missing, though, is anything that we recognize as passion. There are no Romeos and Juliets; no one is dying for, or saved by, another's love.

When our anthropologists inquired into why this is the case, they began to get a clearer picture of the conventions governing the aliens' sexual behavior. It takes place in a society free of any concerns about who does what with whom, so long as the activity is consensual and does not harm others. Questions about divine law, monogamy, homosexuality, or "non-standard practices" were met with incomprehension. Indeed, it was striking how experimentation is generally encouraged. "But what if one's partner doesn't like the new ways?" an earthling naturally asked. This was when the bomb dropped.

"If someone ceases to enjoy the changing tastes of one's partner, he or she simply hires another one. Or several." This reply was almost as startling to the earth scientists as the aliens' initial appearance. After a renewed round of studies gathered and crunched bigger and bigger data, the anthropologists' suspicions were confirmed. The basis for all sexual activity on the planet was commercial. Everyone bought and sold sex. To prepare themselves for this trade, schoolchildren took mandatory courses in erotic technique and advertising.

Some who discovered that they had a special aptitude went on to major in the subject as undergraduates and graduates. Equipped with degrees from the most prestigious universities, their professional services commanded the highest fees. No tycoon or politician was without his or her ivy-league doctor.

The scientists strove to understand this state of affairs objectively and non-judgmentally. Predictably, though, news of their findings caused a sensation back home. Some on earth could not wait to tour the planet and one university even raced ahead to open a branch campus on its soil. Most people, however, exhibited the opposite reaction. They were stunned that an entire civilization could run on prostitution. As their surprise curdled into disgust, fanned by the usual opportunists, louder and louder voices demanded that the aliens vacate our planet. Religious fanatics and conservative moralists joined artists and romantics on the left in denouncing the barbarians who did not even know what love is. How could we expose our sons and daughters to their heartless and dehumanizing ways? Soon enough, a shrewd TV personality rode this outrage to political power. When he took office as world president, he swore he would deport the aliens and build an interstellar wall.

Before he could act, though, the president was summoned to the alien embassy. And before he could deliver his carefully polled statement of principle, he was unceremoniously told that the aliens were leaving. And that they prohibited all further contact with them.

As the alien researchers on earth packed up their gear, they were asked by their earth colleagues about what had spooked the people and leaders of their planet. One alien shook her head sadly. "It was your, let us say, 'strange' approach to education. Believe me, the true scholars among us wanted to understand more about how it works and developed. But when most of our people got wind of what you were doing to yourselves and especially to your young, they flipped. No offense, but they didn't want to risk you contaminating their kids."

She explained that when they looked at how the term *education* was used on earth, they saw that it was defined by a specific practice. In it, someone acquires propositional knowledge or practical know-how; this person is called a learner. When someone else helps the learner gain such knowledge, this person can evidently demand a fee for this service, not to mention a degree of deference, for which he or she is accountable. At the center of this exchange, then, is the learner's satisfaction. "Now we also use the word *learning* to describe the activity of acquiring knowledge," the anthropologist went on. "For us, it usually does play a part in an education, although it would be considered rather pathetic to have to pay for it. But when education is identified with this one practice entirely, when the devotion we have for the life of education is reduced to the transient pleasures of just learning, pleasures that a market fastens on to and exploits, well, we can't help but feel that something sacred to our culture has been trashed. And we have a word—a rather insulting one, I'm afraid—for those who encourage, profit from, and service this reduction: *teachers*."

* * *

How could there be a dimension of education distinguished from learning? And how could this dimension be so important to us that failure to appreciate it could be considered reasonably akin to mistaking prostitution for love? These are the central questions of this book.

Now as my opening recourse to science fiction suggests, it is hardly obvious that these questions have a basis in fact. Looking at the real world rather than a made-up one, one might see no reason to suspend disbelief that education and learning can be separated. Setting aside any entertaining fantasies, can I point to anything that might lend at least initial plausibility to the idea of education without learning?

Consider the etymology of the verb *to educate*. It is rooted in the Latin term *dūcere*, which may be translated as "to lead." It links together a number of English words with the same ancestry such as *abduct, adduce, conduct, deduce, duct, induce, introduce, produce, reduce,* and *seduce*.[1] As *educate* takes its place in this family, it is related to two further Latin constructions: *ēdūcere*, meaning to lead out, as one might lead forth troops, and *ēducāre*, meaning to bring up, to rear, to nurture, as one might children or domestic animals.[2] Fast forwarding to our day, the virtual conflation of education with learning suggests that what it means to educate someone has become predominantly associated with *ēducāre*. Current common sense tells us that in order to foster

---

[1] See *The Oxford Latin Dictionary, Second Edition*, ed. P. G. W. Glare (Oxford: Oxford University Press, 2012), 632–34; and Michiel de Vaan, *Etymological Dictionary of Latin and the other Italic Languages* (Leiden: Brill, 2008), 181.
[2] See *The Oxford Dictionary of English Etymology*, ed. C. T. Onions, with the assistance of G. W. S. Friedrichsen and R. W. Burchfield (Oxford: Clarendon Press, 1966), 301.

the growing up of youths, we need to help them acquire crucial knowledge and know-how. For all practical purposes, the ties between *educate*, *ēdūcere*, and *dūcere* are downplayed if not entirely forgotten.

Now in contrast, I want to elucidate the side of education that is not learning by pursuing the possibility that *ēdūcere* cannot be, in effect, reduced to *ēdūcāre*. Could it be that the experience of being led out, unlike that of being brought up or reared, does not depend centrally on the acquisition and stockpiling of knowledge? Could this experience be, nevertheless, crucial for a meaningful life? How could schooling better serve this other education?

Ēdūcere implies, on the one hand, some kind of movement outward, and on the other, something that guides it. If we think of ourselves as the ones being educated, we may understand this movement to be that of living our lives. As for the guide, one could take it to be a form of knowledge, but this would be to define its nature and status prematurely and unnecessarily. A more carefully neutral way of characterizing what leads us out, one that allows for the possibility that we may live our lives well without claiming to possess a particular knowledge, is as a sort of path. Accordingly, there is something in education that pertains specifically to the experience of finding one's sense of direction. My book aims to do nothing more, and nothing less, than to spell out the implications of taking this seriously. Since we continue to employ the term *education* and invest it with serious concern, it is reasonable to hypothesize that at least traces of this part of its original meaning are still understood to make a significant difference in our lives. If only superficially, associated terms like *course* and *curriculum* echo the theme of leading out. I hope to draw out a richer and deeper sense in which this theme remains vital. At the same time, given that *education* is now usually taken by us to refer to schooling in which the concern for *ēdūcāre* and learning is paramount, I want also to examine what we may be missing when we forget or neglect the experience of being led out. My likening of education as only learning to prostitution is meant to be more than just a provocative trope. I hope to persuade readers that it broaches a fruitful way to understand why and how our practices and institutions of learning may awaken, despite their ever-increasing sophistication, a longing for something else entirely.

Something about being led out was once thought to be good for us; in the course of developing a stable place for it, however, educators and education stakeholders began to stress more and more learning. Now I am not in a position to recount a history of why and how this shift in meaning and behavior took place. My much more modest goal is simply to discern where in our culture at present an appreciation for leading out still exists and to consider why and how this appreciation should be cultivated. Motivating my inquiry, which is more future than past oriented, is thus the belief that there exist latent possibilities in our current culture for reviving and advancing education as leading out. In tune with this book's opening, much of the time I will be speaking in an unabashedly speculative voice. The exploratory nature of my thinking is what makes this work an essay.

Of course, the fact that it seeks to imagine a path to a particular future does not absolve it from having to establish a persuasive degree of plausibility. I welcome responsibility for taking into account evident obstacles to any such path. Some hurdles, to be sure, will come into view only when hypotheses about the way forward are methodically put to the test by empirical research. I acknowledge that my proposals for how to cultivate a future for education as leading out will thus remain liable to being tripped up by such findings; part of what I want to signal when I call my study speculative is a humility about this vulnerability and about my work's preliminary nature. That aside, I am nevertheless confident that I can develop proposals that do not run afoul of features of our commonsense world and I accept that as the burden of my argument. Furthermore, I believe I can best do this by pursuing a line of thinking that is as coherent and comprehensive as possible. The more I can weave together relevant features of our ordinarily recognizable situation with a working-out of the implications of taking the idea of education as leading out seriously, the less likely will my proposals be to contradict what is practically possible. Stitching together the familiar and the speculative will be my responsiveness to the questions that each realm raises for the other. It is the promise that such a disciplined line of theorizing holds out that directs me to conduct this study in a philosophical fashion.

A philosophical theory of the nature of education as leading out, of why it is important, and of how we may cultivate it in our current situation: these are the aims of my inquiry. Now where do I look for answers to these questions?

*　*　*

In road movies, the title to this book declares. Admittedly, this sounds whimsical. But here is why I want to pursue this lead seriously.

The part that can seem like fanciful word play is the association of *ēdūcere* (to lead out) with the concept of the road as something that leads out. Such a link seems to ignore the fact that the corresponding Latin word for road, *via*, has no marked connection with *ēdūcere*. Moreover, an anthropologist from our opening tale would be apt to caution us that in order to understand a word, we have to do more than attend to its resonances with other words in a dictionary. We need to observe how the word is actually used and woven into a network of activities. Hence this anthropologist might turn critic and complain that the association between *education* and *road* is too free because it is an artifact of rather selective and decontextualized translations of Latin into English.

This objection would shut down my line of speculation in the name of linguistic correctness. My defense against it is to suggest, instead, that we acknowledge the "poetry" of the association, yet treat this poetry not as a sloppy violation of some rule but as a fortuitous intimation of some new possibility for us. The substance and value of this possibility, like the proverbial pudding, will only be proven when it is eventually eaten, or at least distinctly tasted. For this reason, the poetry asks us to take it as prophetic of a fuller philosophical understanding down the road and calls for some patient faith in its payoff. Some readers may recognize in this suggestion the example of Martin Heidegger, whose work employs etymologies as a guide for questioning, however controversial his answers (particularly in the realm of politics) remain.[3] Regardless of whether you believe that his claims are in the end justified, his work demonstrates that a kind of philosophical thinking may take flight once we deliberately and carefully relax our strictures against poetry. To be sure, at some point, we will each have to judge whether this relaxation is worth the insights it gives us access to. I am not at all advocating linguistic license for its own sake. My plea is simply that we do not rush to this judgment at the very start.

Suppose that we conceive of education as leading out. Or rather, let me put this more precisely because I want to dwell on the directly first-person, experiential nature of education: suppose that we conceive of it as someone's experience of being led out. How might our experiences of roads that analogously lead out shed light on the nature of education? In pursuit of this

---

[3] For one instance among many of this approach, see Martin Heidegger, *What Is Called Thinking?* trans. J. Glenn Gray and F. Wieck (New York: Harper and Row, 1968).

question, I shall scrutinize a kind of experience that is registered in a phrase with wide currency: the experience of "being on the road." To be educated is to be on the road: What might this mean? Why might this be good for us?

If we are willing to follow the path of this inquiry, the pertinence of the cinematic genre known as the road movie should not seem so outlandish. These kind of works feature film records of actual road travel, often shot and edited in a fashion that amplifies the magnitude of the voyage. Around this footage, a fictional story is constructed that invests the travel with dramatic and at times philosophical significance. The films show us stories of how road travel makes a crucial difference to its characters. My hunch is that at least some of these stories also reveal how education takes place and matters.

* * *

Of course, I have been introducing the road movie in a very abstract fashion. When we consider actual examples of the genre, we may be less confident that they offer us much insight into education. Think of the murderous, ultimately self-destructive outlaws portrayed in films like *Bonnie and Clyde* (1967), *Badlands* (1973), *Wild at Heart* (1990), *Natural Born Killers* (1994)—the list goes on. Are they the fruits of leading out? How plausible is it to associate the hopes we traditionally invest in education with the horrifying nihilism splashed on the screen by these flicks?

Moreover, with these doubts in mind, one might contend that a more promising way to explore the link between education and the road is to turn, instead, to the tradition of literature that features the theme of journey. From the *Odyssey* and *The Divine Comedy* to *The Adventures of Huckleberry Finn* and, of course, *On the Road*, there is no shortage of classic texts that subject the experience of traveling to the most thoughtful, indeed educational, examination. Why not focus the study on such widely celebrated works of high culture instead of ones that are often shameless about their exploitation of sensationalism?

I am going to be answering these two sets of questions over the course of this book. For now, I can aver that these concerns help explain why the book's central object of study is the road movies specifically of Wim Wenders. Wenders is one of the most distinguished filmmakers working in our time. At the moment of this writing, he has directed over 30 feature-length films. (This book was completed before *Submergence* (2017) was released in the United

States; this film is not considered in the discussion that follows.) These include *Paris, Texas*; *Wings of Desire*; and *Buena Vista Social Club*, works that received, respectively, the 1984 Cannes Golden Palm, the 1987 Cannes Best Director Award, and the European Film Award for Best Documentary in 1999. In 2015, Wenders was celebrated at the Berlin Film Festival with an Honorary Golden Bear for lifetime achievement in cinema. Besides his films, he has authored numerous essays and pieces of film criticism and has produced an impressive body of photography, exhibited in galleries and museums such as the Museum Kunstpalast in Düsseldorf, New York's James Cohan Gallery, and Moscow's Multimedia Art Museum, and collected in over 6 books. In my judgment, even his minor works in these different mediums manifest impressive achievements in craft and originality.

The main reason Wenders is at the center of this study, though, is that he has dedicated most of his cinematic work to the road movie genre. This is emblemized by the name of the long-standing film production company that he runs, Road Movies, which has recently been changed to Neue Road Movies. It is no exaggeration to assert that virtually every film he has made, including works in other genres such as thrillers and documentaries, is inflected by his passion for this genre. And more to the point for my project, his specifically road movie oeuvre adds up to a deeply thoughtful, exploratory revision of the genre.

I claim that Wenders's road movies draw out in a compelling way the educational dimension of travel stories. This argument will develop out of close readings of his chief films in this genre, starting with *Alice in the Cities* (1974). In advance of that interpretive work, I can point to one intriguing piece of evidence that might lend some provisional credibility to my thesis. After the success of *Alice in the Cities*, which Wenders has likened to a moment of personal conversion, he immediately turned, in collaboration with the writer Peter Handke, to a film adaptation of Johann Wolfgang von Goethe's *Wilhelm Meister's Apprenticeship*. This novel is traditionally considered to be the first and model *Bildungsroman*, that is, novel of formation. Out of it grew an established and accomplished literary genre. The fact that Wenders so directly linked his new cinematic calling, his dedication to the road movie, to a classic portrait of *Bildung* or formative education suggests that at the outset of his career he at least sensed the possible educational meaning of travel stories.

As I shall detail in what follows, Wenders provides us with examples of road movies that veer away from conventional tropes of violent criminality on the run in favor of an emphasis on introspective and conversational quest. These films capture the complex and nuanced experiences of its characters in a way that is comparable to the most canonical literature. If there is any truth to the idea that the experience of education resembles the experience of being on the road, his films should enable us to see it.

* * *

This book, then, is going to articulate two principal claims. The first is that education should be understood as an experience of being led out on a kind of road. The second is that it should not be understood to be centered on, let alone reducible to, learning, that is, the acquisition of knowledge, usually from a professional teacher. Concerning this second point, let me be plain: I do not at all deny that projects of learning are crucially important to us. I am insisting only that they do not constitute our entire involvement in education, that our language gains in precision when we keep in view the differences between *education* and *learning*. Hence I prefer to separate these terms. At any rate, in the chapters that follow, I shall try to argue for these positive and negative points in this order. Let me say a few words about why.

We can think up reasons to proceed in the opposite fashion. One tried and true argumentative strategy, represented, say, by Karl Marx's dialectical thinking, is to give voice first to our discontent with the prevailing state of affairs and then to find in that the incentive to look in our current world for seeds of another possible one.[4] Applying this strategy to our study, we could imagine turning first to an examination of what we feel is debilitating about the equation of education with learning. On the basis of this negative assessment, we could subsequently try to propound the argument that latent in this state of affairs is, nevertheless, the redemptive possibility of conceiving of education alternatively as being led out. Developing this possibility would thus represent a solution to the ills rooted in education as only learning. The value of this development would therefore be clear.

Friedrich Nietzsche, though, points to a reason why we should be wary of this strategy. The strategy roots the argument for education as being led out in the experience of suffering. Our commitment to this idea of education flows

---

[4] See Karl Marx and Friedrich Engels, "Manifesto of the Communist Party," in *The Marx-Engels Reader*, ed. Robert C. Tucker (New York: W. W. Norton, 1978).

from our unhappiness with education as only learning and the world the latter fosters. Education as being led out, then, elicits our support because it promises to make us happier. Now on the face of it, this might seem to be the epitome of what a compelling argument should look like and we may wonder how there could possibly be a stronger motivation to adopt an idea. The catch, though, is that this implies we aim above all to be happy; ideas present themselves to us as possibly useful concepts that serve the attainment of that goal. It becomes harder to conceive of ourselves contrariwise as serving an idea, let alone as sacrificing our happiness or even our lives to it. Again, one might think this is as it should be. But at the very least, we know that there are records of, and reflections on, human experience that testify to an opposite kind of heroism. Furthermore, some of these musings have made it more difficult for us simply to assume that we know what happiness is, or that it can be entirely identified with a state of pleasure or comfort.[5]

Nietzsche also observes that when it is a question of happiness, jealousy is never far away. My unhappiness is often compounded with envy for those who appear happier. The same situation that makes me unhappy evidently does not harm others who are in it as well—and that deepens my discontent and hostility to them. Revenge against their privilege, fueled by what Nietzsche calls *ressentiment* or resentment, is thus bound to affect social harmony. Political divisiveness and antagonism become the normal state of affairs.[6]

Pursuing an alternative argumentative strategy that tries to avoid being trapped by these concerns, Nietzsche recalls, calls for, and exercises a different "mode of valuation." Admittedly, he dubs this way of presenting the good of an idea "aristocratic"; at this late date, though, after the lessons of the twentieth century's political struggles, I cannot see any reason to burden the mode with such class associations.[7] Setting them aside, I reconstruct his approach as follows: Lead with the positive idea. Emphasize those features of it that inspire and challenge us to find the power in ourselves to live up to it, to devote ourselves to it. Affirm the possibility of living a life given over to this idea,

---

[5] Much of Nietzsche's critique of our society's preoccupation with happiness is epitomized in his sketch of the figure of the "last man." See Friedrich Nietzsche, *Thus Spoke Zarathustra*, trans. Walter Kaufmann (New York: Penguin, 1954), 16–19.
[6] See ibid., 99–103.
[7] See Friedrich Nietzsche, *On the Genealogy of Morals*, trans. Walter Kaufmann (New York: Random House, 1967), 25–34.

a life in which there is something more important to us than our personal happiness. In other words, claim that we could die meaningfully for the idea, and that this is precisely what is good about it. Once we have done this, we can subsequently address stumbling blocks to such a devotional life not as sources of unhappiness to be eradicated but as challenges to place the idea, like Wallace Stevens's jar, in the world, a struggle we have committed ourselves to and relish.

How would this approach to valuation affect our social fabric? Once more, Nietzsche appears to me to be needlessly, indeed perversely, provocative in his language. In opposition to a society preoccupied with *ressentiment*, Nietzsche imagines one marked by the "pathos of nobility and distance," in which those who are strong enough to devote themselves to an idea look down with superhuman contempt on those who are enslaved to their need for self-preservation.[8] It is hard for me not to see Nietzsche's own spirit of revenge at work in this self-justification. It makes much more sense that someone who is true to an idea would be at peace with others; if anything, the idea would be apt to move her to dedicate herself as well to helping those others find their own capacity for non-resentful self-sacrifice. Along these lines, Alain Badiou's philosophy represents a suggestive confluence of Marxian and Nietzschean currents.[9] In place of Marx's materialist stress on how our thinking is conditioned by our participation in historical modes of production, Badiou insists on the crucial priority for any political struggle, including the one Marx calls for, of a Nietzschean idea. At the same time, he explains that the only social order that would encourage all of us to live in true Nietzschean fashion by an idea, by an affirmative mode of valuation, is a communist one; the idea that inspires our politics should be that of communism. In effect, he corrects for Nietzsche's clinging to the trappings of aristocracy by arguing that the latter's mode of valuation calls us more consistently to reach toward Marx's ultimate vision.

In any case, my expository strategy in this book, if nothing else, is going to be Nietzscho-Badiouian in that it prioritizes a positive idea of education as being led out. My hope is that I can draw out the inspiring meaning of this idea by describing how Wenders's characters respond to it, how their actions and their stories as a whole become intelligible and moving in its terms. If I

---

[8] Ibid., 26.
[9] See, chiefly, Alain Badiou, *Being and Event*, trans. Oliver Feltham (New York: Continnum, 2005).

succeed, we will then have reason to look for practical ways to negate or, more precisely, reform the current regime of learning without education.

* * *

I realize that all this talk of ideas is liable to trigger alarm that my study will obscure the concrete particularities of Wenders's films in a haze of generalities. Indeed, the very idea of looking in these films for a philosophical theory of education may seem a recipe for misreading. Is it not likely that there will be features of these works that resist being understood in this light? How will I resist, for my part, the temptation to downplay or distort those features? By projecting on to Wenders's oeuvre my own framework of understanding rooted in an idiosyncratic set of concerns—so idiosyncratic that I derive them from a world of science fiction and poetry—am I not bound to do an injustice to its autonomy?

I hope it is clear that I do recognize this as a concern. Indeed, I would take it a step further: although Wenders appears in writings and interviews to be entirely comfortable with describing some of his films as road movies, I do not want to take for granted that this is an apt characterization. In fact, although I have already used the term for introductory purposes, I regard it as a matter of conscientiousness for me not to assume that we know in truth what a "road movie" is or how to apply this concept to particular films. I agree that if I simply cooked up on my own a concept of the essence of the road movie, when I turned to the films, I would be prone to see what I want, and not what Wenders wants me, to see. To guard against such solipsism, then, I need to make sure that what a "road movie" means can be convincingly derived from a study of the films with all their individuating differences. My way of trying to ensure the accuracy of this derivation is to construct the concept in a step-by-step, transparent fashion, one that invites readers to check whether the concept's elements really can be found in the films I claim to be drawing them from. It is only after I have in hand a road movie concept that describes persuasively how a group of Wenders's films stand related to each other, that I can confidently go on to consider what this representative for the films, so to speak, has to say about the experience of being led out. Only then can I present it as an idea that may inspire a life of education.

I find guidance for this approach in a passage by the philosopher Stanley Cavell from his book *Conditions Handsome and Unhandsome: The Constitution of Emersonian Perfectionism*. Before Cavell wrote this text, he had developed arguments for the existence of two hitherto unrecognized film genres: the comedy of remarriage, and the drama of the unknown woman. In them, he explains how the constituent films, once they are brought together, enter into a productive conversation among themselves that generates still other related films, which test and elaborate a set of common conventions. At the same time, he scruples against projecting on to these films any preconceptions about their essence, including any confident assumption that they necessarily belong together at all. In the abovementioned book, he similarly explores the possibility and productive value of gathering a number of literary and philosophical texts and works of cinema together into still another, overarching genre, one that he calls "Emersonian perfectionism." Here is how he introduces this project:

> A definition of what I mean by perfectionism, Emersonian or otherwise, is not in view in what follows. Not only have I no complete list of necessary and sufficient conditions for using the term, but I have no theory in which a definition of perfectionism would play a useful role. I emphasize accordingly that an open-ended thematics, let me call it, of perfectionism, which I shall adumbrate in a moment, is not to my mind a mere or poor substitute for some imaginary, essential definition of the idea that transcends the project of reading and thematization I am undertaking here. This project, in its possible continuations, itself expresses the interest I have in the idea. That there is no closed list of features that constitutes perfectionism follows from conceiving of perfectionism as an outlook or dimension of thought embodied and developed in a set of texts spanning the range of Western culture, a conception that is odd in linking texts that may otherwise not be thought of together and open in two directions: as to whether a text belongs in the set and what feature or features in the text constitute its belonging.[10]

Virtually every sentence of this passage is instructive for my project. Like Cavell, I shall decline to define the road movie, that of Wenders's or in general, or to define education. I do not want to proceed as if there were some predetermined, closed set of "necessary and sufficient conditions" for employing these terms correctly. The reason is that if we are seriously willing to entertain the possibility of these terms, via their gradual articulation,

---

[10] Stanley Cavell, *Conditions Handsome and Unhandsome: The Constitution of Emersonian Perfectionism: The Carus Lectures, 1988* (Chicago: The University of Chicago Press, 1990), 4.

opening up a break from the familiar world of education as only learning, then it makes sense that we would be careful not to subject the terms in advance to rules of proper usage that are enforced by and enforce that world. I had already rejected the principle of abiding by such rules when I allowed myself to follow the leads of speculative poetry and science fiction. Instead, my project of "reading and thematization" will chart the experiences portrayed in Wenders's films of being on the road in an "open-ended" fashion, open in particular to the likelihood that either Wenders or someone he has influenced will artistically take these experiences in still other directions, or that critics of my work will find still other resonances in them. Such an open-endedness to this study, I shall eventually if provisionally conclude, precisely reflects and suits the experience of being led out.

Instead of applying to Wenders's films a concept of the essence of the road movie, therefore, I shall approach them with the question of their "family resemblances," to echo Ludwig Wittgenstein's famous term.[11] When I tentatively place certain films next to others under the rubric of the Wenders road movie, I shall try to see if common traits become visible and how those traits relate to other features that differentiate the films. Discerning and sorting out these features will enable me to understand more clearly the nature of these films' family and how it could accommodate still other members with their variations. The Wenders road movie will in this fashion start to emerge as a living genre, however modest in size, and its life may be additionally prolonged and enhanced by expanding the family category to the Wendersian road movie. Indeed, I hope that this reading and thematization work, which concentrates first on a group of pretty much patently related films and then widens its survey to take in ones that less obviously belong together, will eventually take us to works in which the "road" is metaphorical and in which the relations to other family members depend on less literal depictions of being led out. At that point, we will have arrived at the education movie. The possibility of characterizing Wenders road movies in this light as also education movies broaches, too, the possibility of relating them to other works of education in different mediums. It is in this way, then, that an inquiry into Wenders's road movies may eventually place us in a position to establish and

---

[11] Ludwig Wittgenstein, *Philosophical Investigations, Third Edition*, trans. G. E. M. Anscombe (New York: Macmillan, 1958), 32.

elaborate the book's overarching contrast between education without learning and learning without education.

* * *

Let me close this introduction with a sketch of the chapters to come.

What is a Wenders road movie? Chapter 1 breaks ground on this question by focusing on *Alice in the Cities*. I have already remarked that by his own testimony, this film was pathbreaking for Wenders. "With *Alice in the Cities*, I found my individual voice in the cinema."[12] Accordingly, we may surmise that in some ways, at least, his subsequent films have their origins in this one. Starting out from it, then, I shall consider in what sense we may call it a road movie. Does it contain film footage of road travel? How does it weave these sequences with others in order to tell a fictional story about this travel? In particular, how do the main characters in this story find meaning in their journey? This chapter concludes that *Alice in the Cities* raises and answers four questions that enable it to make sense of its journey's turning points: Who is being led out; what characterizes his or her life as a whole? From where is he or she being led? To where is he or she being led? And lastly, who or what is leading the person out? The film's way of addressing these questions makes visible to us that what is at stake in them is someone's destiny.

After I have mapped out a number of *Alice in the Cities*'s features that lead me to call it a road movie, the second chapter turns to the hypothesis that other works of Wenders are marked by similar traits and can be read as extensions of, and variations on, that film. I shall describe in some detail how a selection of these later fiction films expresses its family genes, as it were, yet also departs in proliferating ways from them. Following a heuristic fiction of my own, that of Wenders's calling elaborating itself, I examine these films in chronological order, trying to discern how each maintains some features of its predecessor or predecessors while dropping others and adding new ones. My selection is rather conservative: I have left aside some minor works and some borderline and ambiguous cases. What remains is a sequence of work that gives us a suggestive picture of how the Wenders road movie family grew in signature distinction, refinement, complexity, and reach, all the while maintaining its

---

[12] Wim Wenders, *On Film* (London: Faber and Faber, 2001), 254.

responsiveness to the four questions of *Alice in the Cities* and to the interest in destiny. The films this chapter discusses are *Kings of the Road* (1976); *Paris, Texas* (1984); *Until the End of the World* (1991); *Land of Plenty* (2004); and *Don't Come Knocking* (2005).

These two chapters work out an account of how a series of Wenders's films develops into a recognizable family, one which I call the Wenders road movie. Chapter 3 summarizes its features and probes what these distinguishing traits stand in contrast to. The aim here is to sharpen our understanding of the Wenders road movie by examining what it is significantly not. How do his road movies differ from other road movies? How do they differ from other kinds of work that stress the experience of being led out? I shall tackle the first question by comparing this group of his films to what is arguably the first and model road movie, *Easy Rider* (1969), and to one of his in which the protagonist's destiny is not at stake, *Lisbon Story* (1994). This enables us to start to see how he has revised the genre so that the road draws its travelers into an education. Staying on the theme of travel, I then compare the Wenders road movie to the travelogue film, examining how fictional narrative, more than the rhetoric of nonfictional documentary, enables him to explore the question and meaning of destiny in an especially gripping way. His documentary film *Tokyo-ga* (1985) helps bring this contrast into focus. I next compare his interest in destiny to film noir's stress on tragic fate. A look at the proto-road-movie noir *Detour* (1945) and Wenders's own noir *The American Friend* (1977) illuminates why destiny and fate, far from being synonymous, are in truth opposed to each other. Unlike fate, destiny is necessarily educational. Wenders illuminates this dimension of destiny further when he turns the pioneering *Bildungsroman*, *Wilhelm Meister's Apprenticeship*, into the film *Wrong Move* (1975). This adaptation extends Goethe's portrait of youthful formation into an education that is more closely identified with life in its entirety.

By the time we reach the fourth chapter, we will hopefully have our hands on a plausible concept of the Wenders road movie and on a sense of how that concept illuminates the experience of being led out. This sets the stage for an examination of how the Wenders road movie family develops into something that I call the education movie. I shall turn first to a famous and key work of his that came out in the middle of the road movie sequence traced above: *Wings of Desire* (1987). It recounts the story of an angel who embarks on a journey to become human. Such a figurative, human-making, formative voyage is similarly at the center of three films Wenders made after his last road movie (as of this writing): *Palermo Shooting* (2008), *The Salt of the Earth* (2014), and *Every Thing Will Be Fine* (2015). In these recent pictures, road travel recedes in importance for the story, to be replaced by a stronger sense of metaphorical, educational travel. The protagonists change into new people by discovering and affirming their life paths. At the same time, these education movies remain recognizably related to their road movie ancestors in the director's oeuvre and so may be understood as the culmination of that mini-genre of Wenders.

Chapter 5, then, derives from the features of the Wenders education movie a theoretical concept of education as destiny. At its core, once more, is the possibility that we may each understand our lives as a story of being led out that is responsive to the four questions raised by *Alice in the Cities*. I shall elaborate this idea by exploring one last contrast: that with the idea of education as only learning. Why is the difference between these two ways of understanding education more than just a matter of semantic niceties? How does education as only learning, with its stress on the exchange of commodities, prevent us from appreciating and cultivating the specific good of education as destiny, in the same way that sexual life as only prostitution renders romantic love and its fulfillments inconceivable? In what manner do we, nevertheless, express a longing for that good? This chapter articulates what my study of the experience of being led out in Wenders's films puts at stake for learners and school stakeholders.

The concluding, sixth chapter is a brief coda. It returns to the book's opening fable and simply tries to point out one way we might help grow a culture of education as destiny. I shall suggest that our longing to live a meaningful life, sharpened precisely by our current diet of predominantly education-less school learning, may be connected to inspiring and guiding works of such destiny education in programs of liberal learning. In this fashion, a part of the system of learning could turn to serve this education. For some time now, the traditional project of liberal learning has been under attack for its uncertain market value. I hope that this study will encourage us to defend it in the name of a clear, reasonable, moving human good—and not only defend it, but work to enhance its effectiveness in specific ways for this sake. I end this book essay by imagining a destiny devoted to focusing liberal learning teaching on works of education such as those of Wenders.

I have tried to register some of the limitations of this study at various points in this introduction but now that I have run through the book's argument as a whole, let me quickly acknowledge a couple more. These concern the audiences I would like this work to address. I hope that scholars, not to mention fans, of Wenders's films may be interested in this new, education-oriented, philosophical approach to his oeuvre. This book-length study seeks, as its central aim, to elucidate the thematic and formal unity of his road movies.[13] Admittedly, though, I do not try to cover comprehensively all his works in other genres, nor do I delve very far into the histories and technical details of any of their making. Moreover, I do not argue with the secondary literature on them and try to establish the superiority of my film readings. At the end of the day, the question of what his films are about is subsumed under that of what else education could be. Conversely, I hope to interest educators and philosophers of education, particularly those who are concerned about liberal education, in the promise of cultivating the experience of being led out. My path to achieving this, however, demands that I spend considerable effort on doing justice to a body of film work. Predictably, this limits my capacity to engage here with the literature debating the future of liberal education. I hope, however, that my preliminary study may move others to reaffirm this education and pursue it in new directions so that it makes a pivotal difference to our lives.

---

[13] Compare Martin Brady and Joanne Leal, *Wim Wenders and Peter Handke: Collaboration, Adaptation, Recomposition* (Amsterdam: Rodopoi, 2011); Roger Bromley, *From Alice to Buena Vista: The Films of Wim Wenders* (Westport, CT: Praeger, 2001); *The Cinema of Wim Wenders: Image, Narrative, and the Postmodern Condition*, ed. Roger F. Cook and Gerd Gemünden (Detroit: Wayne State University, 1997); Kathe Geist, *The Cinema of Wim Wenders: From Paris, France to Paris, Texas* (Ann Arbor: University of Michigan Research Press, 1988); Alexander Graf, *The Cinema of Wim Wenders: The Celluloid Highway* (New York: Columbia University Press, 2002); Robert Phillip Kolker and Peter Beicken, *The Films of Wim Wenders: Cinema as Vision and Desire* (Cambridge: Cambridge University Press, 1993); and *Wim Wenders*, ed. Jason Wood and Ian Haydn Smith (London: Axiom Books, 2008).

1

Alice in the Cities

A man is driving a car. A bit later, he is riding in a taxi. Still later, he is on a boat, this time accompanied by a young girl. After some bus and monorail trips, they end up in a different car that he again drives. Throughout these sequences and others from *Alice in the Cities*, the camera intermittently turns from the characters to shoot out of the vehicles' windows or at rest stops. It records passing landscapes in South Carolina, New Jersey, New York City, Amsterdam, Wuppertal, Essen, Oberhausen, Gelsenkirchen, and other places along this movie's road. And it responsively focuses on the smallest, most ordinary incidents chanced upon along the way: a blooming tree waves in the wind; cows graze in a pasture in front of a factory; a woman lifts a veil over her mouth; a boy bicycles on the sidewalk along a row of houses (Figure 1.1). The sheer amount of time and attention that the film devotes to the life rustling around its travelers is striking, particularly compared to most fictional films.

Why is this? What is so interesting about the various places and their happenings that the film's characters and we move through? As I discussed in my introductory chapter, this question broaches the road movie. The term suggests that there is a genre of cinematic, fictional narrative that aspires to provide us with some satisfactory, meaningful answers.

Alice in the Cities, released in 1974 as Wenders's fourth feature film, is his first sustained attempt to develop such a narrative.[1] What always beguiles me about it is that for long stretches, the story barely and only ambiguously exists. Indeed, shortly after the initial scenes, its main protagonist, thirty-one year-old Phillip Winter, confesses that he is unable to construct a story out of his

---

[1] There are aspects of the road movie in two early short films of Wenders's, *Alabama: 2000 Light Years* (1969) and *3 American LPs* (1969), and in his first two features, *Summer in the City* (1970) and *The Goalie's Anxiety at the Penalty Kick* (1971).

Figure 1.1 *Alice in the Cities* directed by Wim Wenders © Filmverlag der Autoren, Munich/Westdeutscher Rundfunk, Cologne 1974. All rights reserved.

photographic images; only in the final scene does he declare that he is now ready to finish the story.[2] As the film takes us from Surf City toward Munich, then, it places us on the road from storylessness to authorship. This is the road I want to map in this chapter, as a first step toward tracing the family features of Wenders's road movies. To do so, I need to respect how the film creates for its movement a mesmerizing state of narrative suspension and I need to resist the temptation to impose a premature story on this movement in the form of a plot synopsis. If I can focus on patiently reconstructing how the film's events and its characters' interactions gradually *turn into* a story, I think I will have a better shot at drawing into view what is at stake in it. This work of Wenders shows us how Phillip comes to find redemptive meaning in the experience of being on the road with the eponymous Alice. This experience leads him, and us, to the question of destiny.

Alice opens with a lingering shot of a plane in the sky. Following it as it flies further away and its engine roar is replaced by music, the camera encounters in the foreground a street sign. Panning down from the sign, we come to a

---

[2] In some published interviews with Wenders and in some of the critical literature on his films, the name of this character is spelled "Philip." I follow Wenders's own rendition of the name which he gives us in his recent book, Wim Wenders, *Instant Stories: 403 Polaroids with 36 Stories** (London: Thames and Hudson, 2017), 76.

deserted beach. There is a cut to a partial reverse-angle shot of a boardwalk and then the camera looks underneath it to find, sitting in the sand, Phillip. He looks unhappy. He lifts his own Polaroid camera to his eyes, takes a picture, and waits for the ejected photograph to develop. We see the beach and then we see him looking at the image of the beach, comparing them. As if to express his disappointment, he starts to sing, in a distinctly sardonic tone, the refrain to The Drifters' "Under the Boardwalk." The next, pulled-back shot discloses that in front of him lies a whole row of such photos, one that echoes the very medium of this picture (Figure 1.2). He picks each up, carefully blows the sand from it, and deposits it in a shoulder bag. He then takes up the bag and walks away.

Like most, I cannot help but greet any film at its start with the question of what it is about. Wenders's answer in this case is remarkable for its combination of leisureliness and concision. Right out of the gate, *Alice* rolls along at an unhurried, even pace that lasts until its close. The film is evidently about this kind of time, one that signals that spectacular swerves and explosions of passion are probably not on the horizon. To borrow David Bordwell's useful term, Wenders starts, and stays, on a "dedramatizing" rhythm that propels us gently forward and hypnotizes us into watching even when nothing much

Figure 1.2 *Alice in the Cities* directed by Wim Wenders © Filmverlag der Autoren, Munich/Westdeutscher Rundfunk, Cologne 1974. All rights reserved.

seems to be happening.³ This does not mean, however, that the time of the film is devoid of emotion, or even, as we shall see, of unforced, non-histrionic drama. The musical theme and the lone jet give the opening a melancholy air and the filmmaker quickly and succinctly roots that feeling in who the film is about. Phillip is in a condition that resembles flight. His behavior on the beach introduces us to the elements of his predicament. He looks at the world from a place of solitude. Rather than missing, and searching for, the company of other people, however, he is focused on his problematic relationship to the very world itself. That relationship has something to do with the fact that his photos of things do not capture reality. More generally, any image of a time and a place, such as that imagined in a song, appears deceptive. This gap between the world and his pictures of the world drives him to redouble his photographic attempts to overcome it. "It just never shows what you saw!" he complains obsessively a few scenes later, glancing down at yet another one of his pictures while on the road.

Some of us may recognize in Phillip the textbook problem of philosophical skepticism: How can I ever know that my experience of the world is true to the way the world really is? I want to steer away from analytical discussions of this, though, in order to pursue how Wenders invests this rather abstract, epistemological conundrum with dramatic significance. After all, most of us go about our lives without giving hardly a thought to something so laughably arcane. When faced with this man preoccupied by it, why do we not simply dismiss him as crazy, or at least as someone who has nothing to say about the pressing, practical challenges of our lives?

What may give us intriguing pause is that Wenders implicates in this problem the very film we are watching. *Alice*, like all fictional work in the medium of cinema, relies on the photographic recording of events at a particular time and place in order to convey its story. This convention establishes what we as viewers may expect from it. If, on the contrary, we find ourselves unable to assume that the film's images *are* images, that they automatically and infallibly depict some (perhaps disguised) part of the world, then whatever story the film tries to tell would be apt to be lost in our perplexity. Consider, for instance, the case of a film recounting the sci-fi tale that opens this book. I could imagine

---

³ See David Bordwell, "Art-Cinema Narration," in *Narration in the Fiction Film* (Madison: University of Wisconsin Press, 1985), 205–33.

the filmmaker employing all kinds of special effects to create the illusion of a shockingly alien planet and society. All of this wizardry, however, trades on my rock-solid understanding that at some level, as the proverb has it, photographs do not lie. On top of all the artful makeup, intricate sets, and lighting trickery, what seals my suspension of disbelief in the portrayed alien is my recognition that this work of cinema by nature documents existence. If I suddenly realize that this is not a photographic work at all, I will be at a loss as to how to compose its nonimages into a story.

Along these lines, *Alice* takes off right from the start from a problem that casts doubt, in modernist fashion, on its very intelligibility as a film. On the one hand, the film announces, as it were, that it is going to tell a story about a man alive to a version of the problem of skepticism. This story promises to make understandable how someone could become preoccupied with the gap between photographs and their objects, and how struggling with this gap could make a meaningful difference to one's life. On the other hand, to the extent the film succeeds at this, it will expose its viewers to this same gap and its self-conscious-making paradoxes. They will be invited to identify with a man who cannot identify with a film character. In this sense, Wenders offers us a story that appears bound to be self-deconstructing; at the same time, that story is directly connected to ours as its viewers. This ingeniously unstable ambiguity is part of its hook.

Returning to that sort of story, then, why is Phillip so upset that his photography fails to capture the real world? Why does he even care about this problem? Some of the reasons emerge in a pair of early scenes. The first one takes place after he has been driving for a while up the coast toward New York. One evening, he pulls into the Skyway Motel to check into a room, draws open the window curtains to disclose the neon signs glowing outside, turns on the television, and collapses exhausted on the bed. The TV is playing a classic film by John Ford, *Young Mr. Lincoln* (1939). Phillip drifts off to sleep and when he awakens, he watches a scene in that movie that is abruptly broken by commercials. "A mind is a terrible thing to waste," intones one; in another, a gregarious man from "sunny Florida" introduces himself so that he can pitch something. These advertising images blend in seamlessly with the signs on the streets. Phillip flies into a rage and smashes the machine on the floor.

This first scene tells us that there is something about television that Phillip hates. The second tells us why. After he has reached New York and defeatedly bought a ticket to return on the morrow to Munich via Amsterdam, the scene opens with him sharing a hotel room for the night with two people whom he had just met earlier in the day: Alice Van Dam, the nine-year-old of the film's title, and her mother, Lisa. Alice is asleep on a couch. Lisa raises her head from her pillow as if she cannot sleep and sees Phillip sitting at the foot of the bed, watching a disjointed montage of images on the TV with the sound off and scribbling in a notebook. She asks about what he is writing. In reply, he reads aloud:

> What is so barbaric about this TV is not that it chops up everything and interrupts it with ads, though that's bad enough. Far worse is that everything it shows turns into advertising too, ads for the status quo. All the TV images come down to the same common, ugly message, a kind of vicious contempt. No image leaves you in peace. They all want something from you.

Phillip detests the feeling that television images, like the billboards and signs we are surrounded by, are always trying to reach inside and manipulate us so that we invest ourselves in the prevailing rules of the game. His suffering is exacerbated by the fact that beyond interrupting the programming, the commercial has become its very form; every program now adopts the rhetoric of selling something, of approaching its mass viewers, including him, as potential suckers. Being a similar medium of moving pictures, can cinema oppose this tendency? Can *Alice*? How? Phillip's photography, not to mention Wenders's filming, may be accordingly understood to be a search for images that resist this whole way of looking at the world. Such images would somehow open up and maintain a respectful distance between the world and the viewer who contemplates it.

Unfortunately, as we have seen at the outset, Phillip's search is not going well. His photos only come up false, which fuels his driving worry that there is no alternative to deceptive pictures and their insinuating tales. This is why the gap between image and reality maddens him. Indeed, when later in the film he tours Amsterdam on a boat, the way the guide frames what he sees in order to sell the city revolts him so much, he has to quit the ride before it is over. It seems to him that nothing exists any longer outside the television set.

Moreover, this is not the only thing Phillip quits. It turns out that he is a journalist who has been given the assignment of writing a story on the American landscape. We learn this when he shows up at his editor's New York office empty-handed. The editor angrily interrogates him about what has gone wrong; Phillip explains that as he traveled, the images he saw changed him. As a result, he was impelled to take notes on them and to take plenty of his own photographs, but he has stopped working on any sort of story. He promises to turn these notes and photos into one once he is back in Munich but the editor washes his hands of the entire project; he evidently does not believe that this photo maniac is any longer capable of storytelling. Correspondingly, we may start to become dubious that Wenders's initial series of scenes in *Alice*, with their haphazard shots of the road and their rants against the transformation of life into spectacle, will ever crystallize into much of a narrative. Both Phillip and Wenders have taken us on a trip away from any kind of story.

The first part of *Alice*, then, follows Phillip on his journey to and around New York. He is a man who has become alienated from the land through which he travels by its inescapable, invasive images that assault him. They are relentlessly trying to guide him toward their products. He attempts to defend himself by producing his own counterimages, but they invariably lack truth. Consequently, the real world, off in the distance, ends up leading him on by eluding him and he has become sick of the trip. On top of it all, his very ability to give story form to his life is blocked. Why is this? Perhaps it is because he has come to realize that putting the moments of his life in the service of a story is akin to using images as a sell. He cannot bring himself to participate in this kind of exploitative and distorting betrayal: something about his experience of the here-and-now as such, in its vivid integrity, calls to him to be preserved. Although he always fails to capture it, he senses that truth exists there, in the instant. Like many, he has been seized by the ethic of living in the moment. Formulating this predicament from another angle, we could say that Wenders's film up to this point poses the question of whether it can avoid being made for TV. Is it possible for it to tell a story—which usually implies the point of view of someone looking back on things that have already happened in order to lead its audience to something like a moral—that is not false but true to the open-ended, present tense of filming? Unlike television, can it open our eyes, rather than blind us, to the way the world simply and sometimes movingly, if unprofitably, *happens*?

Indeed, perhaps this is a good place to note quickly that if one wants to dramatize the contrast between something occurring in the present and a retrospective account of that past event, the medium of narrative cinema is especially fitting. Film records what is happening in the world, rather than what an author remembers has happened. Conversely, if one is interested in road journeys that turn on this contrast, one may have reason to pass over the medium of journey literature. A film that records someone being on the road and then someone recalling being on the road draws the difference more sharply than a novel, like Jack Kerouac's, that reflects on both of these experiences.

A last scene in New York before Phillip does fall into the beginning of a tale sheds light on another dimension of his blockage. Instead of sharing a hotel room with Alice and Lisa, he had hoped to spend the night with a girlfriend, Angela. The scene begins when he knocks on Angela's door in spite of the fact that she seems to have been ignoring his phone calls. She lets him in and he begins to talk about his journey. Once he set forth from New York, he recounts, everything looked endlessly the same. Lacking any distinct destination, it became impossible even to imagine anything changing. He drove and drove and progressively got lost, losing touch with himself as well. Angela puts her hand to her head as she listens, as if she has heard this lament many times in the past. She may even derive some dark humor from how it ironically echoes her problem with him. Finally, she breaks into his monologue to remind him that he had already lost himself long before he got to America. And it is for this reason, she points out, that he is constantly taking photos. He is seeking proof that he exists and has experienced something; this reassurance is what he is looking for, too, from other people. But in the long run, nothing and no one can give him that. She tells him, therefore, that he cannot stay with her, that he has to leave. "I don't know how to live either. No one has shown me either."

This exchange places Phillip's predicament in the framework of a relationship and illuminates its meaning for his part in it. His traveling to a strange country and his photography, Angela perceives, amount to a way to prove to himself that his moment-to-moment experiences are special, have substance, and will not merely disappear like a mirage. Insightfully, she understands that the reality eluding him is not that of the world, as he may think, but that of his self. By collecting photos of these experiences, he is trying to possess himself, possess a self. But such a preoccupation leads only to self-centeredness. He may bring his experiences to her, looking for her help in understanding them and in living them out, but he is utterly blocked from receiving her or existing in a relationship with her. From her as well, then, he has to keep moving on.

This predicament of Phillip, which Wenders pieces together during the first, almost nonnarrative third of the film, sets Phillip up for a sequence of events that starts to place him in a story. He runs into Alice. They momentarily trap each other together in a revolving door (Figure 1.3). The comic tenor of this encounter resounds throughout the rest of the film as a counterpoint to the film's melancholy musical theme. After they are both released from the door into the hall of a travel agency, they are tied together in a more serious way by the challenge of getting back to Germany in the middle of a flight controllers' strike. He helps her and her mother book a reservation on the same flight to Amsterdam that he is taking; he also helps them find a hotel room for the night in Manhattan which, as I mentioned, he ends up staying in as well after Angela kicks him out. Following that night, Lisa steals away in the morning to visit her husband, Alice's stepfather, from whom she and Alice are running away. She leaves a note for Phillip and Alice saying that she will rendezvous with them later on the roof of the Empire State Building. After waiting for her there, Phillip sees through a telescope that she is departing from the hotel with her suitcase. He takes Alice back to that place and the manager passes to him another note from Lisa. This one explains that because her husband is distraught, she cannot leave him just yet and has to stay temporarily to calm him down. She pleads with Phillip to take Alice with him to Amsterdam; this

Figure 1.3 *Alice in the Cities* directed by Wim Wenders © Filmverlag der Autoren, Munich/Westdeutscher Rundfunk, Cologne 1974. All rights reserved.

will make it possible for Lisa to tear herself away for good and meet them there the following day.

Without intending to, Phillip has gotten himself mixed up in the Van Dams' marital crisis. One domino is causing another to fall in rapid succession. Barely grasping what is happening, he suddenly has a role in that story and has to act. He follows Lisa's directions and brings Alice along on his flight to Europe. Why does he do this? Why did he not simply leave Alice with the hotel manager or in the care of the police? The answer is far from clear. Part of it may be that he and Lisa are mildly attracted to each other. Rather than checking into his own room in the hotel, he came to her room; she responded that she could not sleep with him but that she would like them to share the bed. It is possible that the prospect of pursuing something with her in Amsterdam vaguely appeals to him, although he does warn her when they first meet that he is not feeling very social. Another possibility is that in his state of being utterly directionless, Lisa's words offer him the momentary relief of a small sense of purpose. Because he is going to Amsterdam anyway and because Alice already has her ticket, traveling in her company would hardly cost him anything. Yet, by deciding to do this, he at least enjoys the feeling of acting to achieve a distinct aim. Whatever the specific reason, this, then, is the first turning point in his journey.

Since Phillip plays along with his role in the Van Dam story, he ends up with Alice in Amsterdam. As I described earlier, a brief tour of the city sours his mood and he and she begin to bicker. When they return to the airport the next day to meet Lisa, she does not show up. He starts to conduct Alice to some officials who could look after her and look for her mother, but she suddenly breaks away and locks herself in a restroom stall. He begs for her to come out but she refuses, weeping. Desperate to resolve the situation, he reminds her that she had earlier expressed a wish to see her grandmother; he asks her about where the latter lives. Although at first she is unable to remember, he runs through a list of German cities until one rings a bell. By consenting to take her to Wuppertal, he cajoles her into leaving the stall. She does not know exactly where in that city her grandmother's house is, but she will recognize it when she sees it.

Once more, these actions on Alice's and Phillip's part raise the question of motivation. Why does she stubbornly refuse to wait any longer for her mother in Amsterdam? And why does he offer to transport her to her Wuppertal grandmother? In the case of Alice, an answer is not hard to figure out. She feels painfully abandoned by her mother; it may be that her real father has also left her with the feeling that she has been deserted. Understandably, she may have seized up at the notion that if Phillip as yet another surrogate father were to ditch her, it would be the last straw. Besides, we may conclude, the possibility that she is acting on unthought-out impulses makes perfect sense: after all, she is only a child. As for him, he may have been motivated by both panic at having to deal with another's emotional meltdown—his own temper, as shown in his breakup with Angela, is very much the opposite—and comfort at doing what is second nature to him: getting back on the road. Moreover, who is to say that he is not rather childish himself? Indeed, I want to suggest that the psychology of these characters is something that Wenders is rather casual about and uninterested in. For the purposes of this emerging narrative, the characters could just as well be children moved by primitive impulses and problematic judgments. I hope to explain shortly why the focus of the story is not on motivation but something else.

In any event, this scene is the film's second turning point. Until he left for Europe, Phillip's road travel was pretty much solitary and aimless. He wandered by himself around America, lost. His arrival in Amsterdam marks the start of a transition: he is still lost but no longer alone. When he and Alice depart that city, they are no longer wandering but are on a quest. More precisely, they are on her quest in which he has enlisted to help her. After following Lisa's directions, he now accepts a part in Alice's story.

On to Wuppertal they go. When Phillip and Alice arrive, they crisscross the city on a series of monorail trips, looking for Grandmother's home but without success. The next day, with his funds running low, he manages to get a car rental agency to accept some expired Eurochecks and they continue their search in an automobile. One of the most beautiful road sequences occurs at this point: Alice struggles to stay awake as she gazes out of the window; he occasionally turns from his driving to glance worriedly at her; both her dreaminess and his sinking feeling of being lost again find lyrical expression in Can's film score. Eventually, they pull into a café in which, in one of the film's most famous shots, a boy is humming along and tapping his feet to Canned Heat's "On the Road Again" playing on the jukebox. They sit at a nearby table and Alice confesses that Grandmother does not live in Wuppertal. Phillip, suspecting that she has known this all along, is furious. "Do you think I'm keen on driving around with little girls and spending my last dime? God knows I've got other things to do." She questions this, observing that all he does is scribble in his notebook, but he makes up his mind to turn her in to the cops. They part coldly at the police station.

Leaving the station, Phillip is, indeed, back on the road. On a whim, he goes to a Chuck Berry concert; he watches the man sing "Memphis, Tennessee." After the concert is over and he parks at his hotel, his car's passenger door is suddenly flung open and Alice gets in. She has escaped from the police and now knows where Grandmother really lives. He laughs helplessly—then tells her that in that case, they better get going.

This is turning point three in the film. I understand it to show Phillip turning away from any worry about making the right decision or about being led on by little girls, let alone media images of them. (Regarding the latter, he even sings out jubilantly into the night the Berry song mentioned above about a man looking for a six-year-old girl.) Instead, he resolves to take responsibility for accompanying Alice regardless of where the journey will lead or what it will cost. He has come to realize that she matters to him; at the concert, he missed her. Seconding his earlier, in-the-heat-of-the-moment offer to help her that he made at the Amsterdam airport, he now affirms the whole road broached by this realization. This, and nothing else, is what he has to do. He seems accepting even of the possibility that this is a play road in some kind of game of hers.

As I suggested earlier, I think this interpretation of this moment places less emphasis on what may be motivating Phillip and more on his existential capacity, which he at last decides to exercise, to commit himself wholly to any course of action like this one. That said, let me, nevertheless, offer an explanation of what he may sense is at stake in Alice's company, of why he may believe it makes a difference to his life; this explanation does shed light on what may be motivating him. It is not psychological, though. I acknowledge that these days, as the news continues to be filled with nauseating reports of one pedophilic crime after another, we are prone to feel creepy about any story in which a man attaches himself to a young girl. In my view, Wenders challenges us to suspend this natural reaction and the psychology it implies in the name of a more vital reason that this particular man might treasure the company of this particular girl. We see this reason in one of the very few shots in the film that is distinctly from Alice's point of view. From the top of the

Empire State Building, she is looking through a telescope at the city; suddenly, she catches sight of a white bird and follows it as it takes its time gliding over the streets and across the sky between the skyscrapers (Figure 1.4). Then the time on the telescope runs out and she asks Phillip for another coin. Setting aside its humorously anticlimactic ending, I find this shot to be, quite simply, the most breathtaking in the entire film. It reveals that Alice is alive to the *appearing* of things in the world. They show themselves to her from the right, respectful distance, figuratively speaking, and she wants nothing more than to wonder at and delight in them. Even in the midst of their comedy of errors, it makes sense that Phillip, who is largely dead because of the way the world merely seems to be, would be impressed by her fresher vision. My explanation for why he wants to be with her is thus in the deepest sense aesthetic: it is about what she shows him of the redeeming power of beauty. This is the reason he now makes her quest story his own.

Leaving Wuppertal, Alice explains that the police figured out her grandmother lives in the Ruhr region. At a rest stop the following morning, Phillip feels daunted by the challenge of finding Grandmother's needle in this region's haystack, especially on the heels of their recent failure. He brightens, though, when Alice produces a photo of Grandmother's home. All they have to do is to find the house that matches the picture. They proceed to drive around and around the area, asking people they run into if they know the location of

Figure 1.4 *Alice in the Cities* directed by Wim Wenders © Filmverlag der Autoren, Munich/Westdeutscher Rundfunk, Cologne 1974. All rights reserved.

the place the photo depicts. A taxi driver suggests they try Erdbrücken Street in Gelsenkirchen.

That is where they find it. "This can't be!" exclaims Phillip, as he looks from the house Alice recognized to the photo. And no wonder he is incredulous: his roaming in the States was driven by his fixation on the mismatch between image and reality. Now they suddenly coincide. What has changed?

A key difference, I find, concerns how the photographs are used. As I explained, Phillip was utilizing the ones he was taking to prove to himself that his experiences matter, that their moments do not just fade away, that their independent life can resist being assimilated into some manipulative, made-for-TV story. In contrast, the photo of Grandmother's home was likely passed on to Alice by a relative; she was utilizing it, with Phillip's help, to find her family again. Phillip's photos are of a strange land that threatens to dispossess him of himself. Alice's photo is of a home that promises to link her to other people. However surprising it is to Phillip, it would appear that when the image and the reality are of home, they are bound to meet. This may be because their true point of contact is not the photograph but a sentiment.

It turns out, though, that this sentiment is not bound to any historical place. After rushing to the house when she spots it, Alice returns to the car dejected: not Grandmother, but an Italian lady, currently lives there. This time, without any exasperation, Phillip rises to the occasion: he proposes that he and Alice go swimming at a nearby pool. After playing in the water, she teases him about looking like her father. She impulsively asks a woman sunbather if she thinks he is her father; this leads to the woman taking them to her place for the night. When Alice arises the next morning, she discovers him and the woman sleeping together. With a touch of jealousy, Alice puts on a dress rather than her usual pants and shirt and after quietly awakening him, she pleads with him to leave his slumbering companion and get back on the road with her right away. Generously and reassuringly, even cheerfully, he acquiesces. In effect, he passes the test of the "other woman" and proves to Alice that he is, if not her father, family. In response, she sprawls out, at home in his car. This is how the road has led him finally to exist. His problematic relationship to the world has been healed by his relationship to her.

Where do they go now? Alice has no further ideas and Phillip decides that they should journey to his parents' home, as if he wants to take this orphaned child into the care of his family. They drive the car on to a ferry boat that is crossing the Rhine. For only the second time since the sojourn in Amsterdam, he takes out his camera; perhaps this is spurred by the voice of a woman singing around him. When he looks in the direction of the mermaid-like figure, he sees the singer holding a boy with Alice standing nearby; their figures are lined up vertically like a totem. Phillip snaps their picture (Figure 1.5). Alice, it appears, has found a mother and a brother to be with. And Phillip, absent in the photo, is nevertheless implicated in it, regarding this group as if it were a family and he were, indeed, the father. To repeat: in this precise sense, he *looks* like a father.

The moment Phillip takes that picture, the moment he feels moved to take it, he is found. This is the last turning point in the story, the one that ends the quest. Coming up from behind, a detective, having recognized Phillip, accosts him and quizzes him about why he disappeared with Alice when he had made it a point to deposit her at the station in the first place. All this time, ironically, the cops have been searching for them; they have already located the grandmother and the mother. The policeman announces that he is going to take Alice to the nearest railroad station and put her on a train to Munich where her family members are waiting; he politely orders Phillip to follow them in his car.

Munich is where Phillip was heading after he admitted the defeat of his writing project in New York and before he met Alice. He no longer has any

Figure 1.5 *Alice in the Cities* directed by Wim Wenders © Filmverlag der Autoren, Munich/Westdeutscher Rundfunk, Cologne 1974. All rights reserved.

money, however. At the train station, he is about to say goodbye to Alice when she solemnly pulls out of her purse a hundred dollar bill and gives it to him. Evidently, she was hanging on to it for emergencies and he now needs it.

The film's denouement takes place on the train. In a compartment, Phillip is reading a newspaper report about the death of John Ford; its headline is "Lost World." From the opposite seat, Alice asks about what he is going to do in Munich. He responds: "I'm going to finish writing that story." He asks her the same question in turn. She shrugs her shoulders and gets up to go to the window. With his help, she opens it and they look outside together. The film cuts to a shot of them from high above in what must be a helicopter. As the music rises, the helicopter does, too, and the camera contemplates for a long moment the train and the vast landscape through which it is passing, before the image fades to black.

It is one thing for Phillip to be pulled into a sequence of events that puts Alice in a jam. It is another for him to realize that he can not only play a role in her struggle to free herself, but also write its story. What brings him to this realization? Perhaps it is the memory of a model storyteller. Since it was what they did to a Ford film that first caused his sickness about television ads to boil over, I think the news of the director's death may have particular resonance. This is furthermore suggested by some remarks about that man's work that Wenders made a couple of years prior to making *Alice*:

> I miss the friendliness, the care, the thoroughness, the seriousness, the peace, the humanity of John Ford's films; I miss those faces that are never forced into anything; those landscapes that aren't just backgrounds; those stories which, even if they're funny, are never foolish; those actors who are always playing different versions of themselves.[4]

It is not hard to see Wenders emulating these same qualities in his own filial film. Likewise, Phillip too may be feeling inspired to write a Fordian story by what he misses.

For such a purpose, moreover, he has stumbled on to a useful vehicle: the episodic form. Phillip's discovery of this occurs in a scene in Wuppertal in which he and Alice have retired to a hotel room following their initial failure to find Grandmother. Alice is crying in bed; he reacts this time with anger.

---

[4] Wenders, *On Film*, 55.

Catching himself, he tries more soothingly to console her and she requests that he tell her a bedtime story. At first, he protests heatedly that he does not know any stories, but catching himself again, he proceeds calmly to make up one on the spot. It goes as follows:

> Once there was a little boy who had gotten lost. He'd gone for a walk in the woods with his mother on a beautiful summer afternoon. When they came to a clearing where the sun was shining, his mother suddenly felt tired and wanted to rest. All of a sudden the boy heard a rustling in the bushes and he discovered a hedgehog. He followed the hedgehog until he came to a stream. And in the stream he saw a fish. He walked along the stream for a long time until he reached a bridge. On the bridge he saw a horseman. The horseman sat very quietly on his horse and looked into the distance. The boy went up to the bridge and walked cautiously around the horse. Then the horseman rode slowly away. The boy followed him until he lost sight of him. And he reached a big road. On the road there were many trucks. The boy waited on the roadside until a truck stopped. The driver asked him if he needed a ride. The boy was delighted. He was proud to sit next to the driver who let him turn the dial on the radio. And the boy drove with him until they reached the sea. And at the sea he remembered his mother.

In this tale, one episode clearly and distinctly follows another, with minimal overlap between them. In particular, each experience appears to generate one action, and vice versa; none exerts much future influence beyond that. Obviously, this is a very primitive story form that lacks any role for accumulated, contradictory, long-term psychological complexes. What it emphasizes, instead, are holistic images of specific happenings. This kind of story does knit events and actions together and does invite us to understand these links in terms of cause and responsibility, but it does not do this at the cost of obscuring what I have called the appearing of the world. For each episode is a moment of this appearing. (Compare, in this respect, the sequence of moments staged in William Carlos Williams's classic poem, "The Red Wheelbarrow.")[5] In the course of contriving this tale, then, Phillip constructs a form that would enable him to tell his larger story without betraying its moments for rhetorical gain. This is evidently the kind of story that Wenders also attempts to film.

---

[5] See William Carlos Williams, "The Red Wheelbarrow," in *The Selected Poems of William Carlos Williams* (New York: New Directions, 1968), 30.

Furthermore, this particular bedtime tale leads at the end to Mother. I do not think it is merely lazy sentimentality that is behind Wenders's stress on the theme of reconstituting family. (Or solely the profound influence on him, to which he has repeatedly testified, of the filmmaker Yasujiro Ozu: Ozu's chief theme in his later work is the disintegration of the family in modern Japan.) I root the focus on family in a concern about audience. Stories are always told *to* someone. What enabled Phillip in Wuppertal to produce even a rudimentary story is the person he related it to, who asked for it. The story that he will be writing in Munich may not be addressed specifically to Alice. But the familial feelings he develops for her may be leading him to an audience that calls for his story.

Now I want to be careful not to understand this too literally, which would sink the film in a bathetic and even dangerous cliché. What saves Phillip's story from being one about rejecting America in order to celebrate the Fatherland to which he and his kin belong is a subtler sense of what family means. It is not at all about having the same blood. When he was drawn away from his preoccupation with self-possession, he left behind, as well, any interest in basing his identity on anything he possesses. He becomes a father figure to Alice because of what he gives her. Conversely, he does not care for her because she is already family. What leads him out of himself to devote himself to her is the key, animating spirit of his story. It is why the title of this film is not *Phillip in the Cities*.

I propose to call this spirit, conversation. It is the conversation between Phillip and Alice that binds them together into an extended family. At one level, of course, this is a rather banal observation: How else could they have become familiar with each other? In New York, he is initially amused by her riddles; later, down the road, their comic banter expands to take in word games, crazy dreams, her piggy appetite, his stupid misunderstandings, quarrels, recriminations, revels in absurdity, and so on. They thus get used to responding to one another, however different and separate in age they are. Eventually, though, this conversation takes on a life of its own: this is what elevates it to a meaningful force in the story. Phillip and Alice come to understand themselves as, above all, participants in something larger than each other. Who one is, is a matter of how one has been called to respond to someone and how one, in turn, calls someone to respond. It is this essentially call-and-response nature of our lives, I am suggesting, that forms the basis of family in this film. To be a relative, to recognize that another belongs to your family, is to affirm that you, this person, and still others are taking part in a conversation that has no identifiable center or definite boundary.

The story that Phillip realizes he is ready to tell, then, was drawn out of him by this kind of conversation. Once upon a time, he was lost; he had been rendered storyless, and virtually dead to the world, by the swarm of images that invaded him in America. On this wandering road, he ran into Alice. He entered into a dialogue with her, one that was driven by her distress, yet was also intermittently lifted by her vision of the world, one that turned their joint road in Europe into a quest. This quest was resolved when they were found. Her mother and grandmother, aided by the police and, of course, in his own blundering way, Phillip, find and send Alice back into the family. And she, as a seer of the appearing world, finds and sends him back into conversation with all his like who cannot help but feel that that world is their home. Responding to her, he now has something to introduce into the conversation. He can share, among other things, how she has changed him from a bag of elusive experiences into an author. This response will, in turn, call out for responses from still others, ones that extend and strengthen the meaningful existence of this family.

In the end, then, what is *Alice in the Cities* about? How does it show what can be dramatically meaningful about travel and the places to which it leads us? Indeed, from the overarching perspective of this book's project, what does it tell us about the experience of being led out?

The film's story is one of redemption. Phillip is saved from being lost in storylessness by the grace of Alice. Drawn out of himself, her appearing draws him initially into her story and finally, although still provisionally, into authorship. She is able to do this because she sets the moving stage, in her plight and quest, for the beauty of the appearing world in its various places to inspire him. The ordinary incidents accompanying them on their trip, some of which I referred to in the opening to this chapter, start to make visible that he is being given life. His wandering road and his quest road eventually turn into the road of the film's last shot: that of destiny (Figure 1.6). Handke, Wenders's longtime friend and occasional collaborator, once had a character in one of his writings evoke destiny in this way: "He sensed with amazement that he had only now really set out from the place he came from."[6]

---

[6] Peter Handke, "Essay on the Jukebox," trans. Krishna Winston, in *The Jukebox and other Essays on Storytelling* (New York: Farrar, Straus, and Giroux, 1994), 118.

Figure 1.6 *Alice in the Cities* directed by Wim Wenders © Filmverlag der Autoren, Munich/Westdeutscher Rundfunk, Cologne 1974. All rights reserved.

What I call destiny has nothing to do with the sense that the course of one's life is externally predetermined. Destiny is, instead, a story form for each of us to understand and author our lives as a whole. It is distinguished from other kinds of story because it is keyed to the experience of being led out, the experience that I am arguing is at the heart of education. To tell someone, yourself or another, a destiny story is to recall your experiences of being literally or figuratively on the road, of moving helplessly through places that do not hold you, and then to weave them into a narrative about how you arrived at a place in the present that sets a direction for how to live and move affirmatively forward. Such a story cannot be reduced to an analysis that solves a problem which will enable you to come closer to achieving a future end; the very end that motivates this problem-solving already presupposes the story that reveals it. All in all, one's destiny constitutes a response to four questions that we can also specifically address to *Alice*. In order to avoid recapitulating its narrative yet again, I will confine myself to the briefest summary points in answer, simply so that they can throw a bit of additional light on what the questions are asking about.

Who is being led out? In the case of this film of Wenders, it is Phillip, a man who is lost in how his experiences lack substance, coherence, and direction. Being thus lost, he fears for his whole life.

From where is he being led? He is being drawn away from his need for self-possession.

To where is he being led? He is being drawn to devote himself to celebrating his conversational family's homeland.

Who or what is leading him out? The answer, of course, is Alice. But she is not in any strict sense a teacher: she does not *try* to lead him out. What happens is, rather, that Phillip's involvement with her predicament and with her way of responding to it draws his attention appreciatively to the happening of the world.

From this chapter's reading of *Alice in the Cities*, I have derived this set of four questions that characterize the film as a destiny story. When I provisionally call *Alice* a road movie, then, I am making two claims: first, that the film depicts protagonists who are travelers, and second, that it gives dramatic meaning to their experiences of being on the road by weaving them into a story of destiny. If this reading is plausible, I now have a form that I can hold up to other films of Wenders. Do the stories in some of them, particularly those that also feature road travel, resemble *Alice* in being, as well, about destiny? Does the question of destiny, analyzed into the four questions above, apply meaningfully and non-misleadingly to them? How do they build on or depart from *Alice*'s story and its answers? These are the guidelines for my discussion in the next chapter. I hope that examining how these distinctly different films narrate their characters' destinies will enable me to trace out some of the family features of the Wenders road movie.

2

Related Road Movies

The previous chapter explained how *Alice in the Cities* frames its depictions of Phillip and Alice traveling, not always together, from South Carolina toward Munich, with a story about why this trip matters, about how it leads to Phillip's destiny. On the basis of it combining in this fashion travel footage and a destiny story, I have proposed to call it a road movie. In order to test whether this conception of a road movie is utterly singular or whether it applies to other films, then, I turn in this chapter to some of Wenders's other works. I focus on feature films telling complex, fictional stories that do not merely include road trips as ancillary events, but that make sense as being *about* those trips.[1] Can these stories be convincingly read as ones also about a traveler realizing that this road has led to his or her destiny? It appears to me that the answer is "yes" in five films that follow *Alice*: *Kings of the Road*; *Paris, Texas*; *Until the End of the World*; *Land of Plenty*; and *Don't Come Knocking*.[2] By examining each of these works in turn, in chronological order, I hope to persuade readers that the early film's story form is viable, capacious, and flexible enough to convey related stories with their particular variations. All in all, this survey amounts to an argument that the Wenders road movie exists.

Why is this worth establishing? Given the concerns I articulated in my introductory chapter, I believe that the existence of this body of work, and the considerable audience it has attracted, testifies that many of us sense, at least, that there is something pivotal about the experience of being led out. Nothing

---

[1] I set aside two of Wenders's shorts which are definitely about road journeys but which do not feature characters with much dramatic depth: *Arisha, the Bear, and the Stone Ring* (1992) and *Twelve Miles to Trona* (2002).
[2] In one case, the answer is arguably no: *Lisbon Story* (1994). This film's protagonist is on the road but not, it appears, to his destiny. I discuss this exception to my account of the Wenders road movie in the next chapter.

less than our lives are at stake in it. I have pointed out that this sense appears to be present in our original understanding that education comprises *ēdūcere*; it helps explain why some of our predecessors may have affirmed education as a matter of vital importance. Now that our schools are virtually all about *ēducāre* and learning, Wenders's road movies constitute an alternative site where we may think together about the many different ways that the experience of being led out, literally taking place on some road, may turn into one's destiny. My suggestion is that if the Wenders road movie exists, so, too, does an interest in a radically divergent conception of education.

Let me clarify a bit more the terms of my study of these films. I shall be looking to describe how each one makes sense as a road movie and destiny story, thereby establishing its relation to others in the family, as well as how each differs from its relatives in significant ways. My aim is to build a case that this cinematic mini-genre has so far proven its evolutionary fitness and also that it is rich in imaginative possibilities for others beside Wenders to continue to explore. Because my focus is on comparisons between works, I will not be discussing each film in the same detail as I did with *Alice*. Furthermore, because I am principally interested, following the lead of that groundbreaking movie, in the nature of the films' stories, I will for the most part pass over stylistic affinities and differences among the works, including, regrettably, their signature imagery and their astute use of (mainly rock) music. Finally, I shall also abstain from making judgments about their relative aesthetic success. Needless to say, I do find some of them more moving and beautiful than others. The point of this survey, however, is not to demonstrate that I can tell the difference between when Wenders is at the top of his game and when he comes up short. It is to invite all who care about education to take seriously what, I am convinced, this generally accomplished body of film work has to show us.

Because my claims about the Wenders road movie are meant to be empirical, it is crucial that I do justice to the concrete particularities of each film's story. This is why my discussion takes the form of a reconstruction of these stories one by one, minimizing any reliance on preestablished categories. My hope is that as I do this, certain recurring concerns and themes will gradually and verifiably become visible. In this chapter, I shall restrict myself simply to flagging these elements, deferring a fuller, synthetic treatment of them until Chapter 4. The central one is the crucial pertinence of the four questions of destiny raised by *Alice* for understanding the narrative arcs of these pictures, too. As I try to establish this, I take myself to be offering an interpretation, rather than a mere plot summary, of each work for a reader who has watched the film for himself or herself.

* * *

Kings of the Road was released in 1976. Its original, quite evocative, title is *Im Lauf der Zeit* (In the Course of Time). This film is often grouped together with its two immediate predecessors, *Alice* and *Wrong Move* (which I shall also put off discussing until the next chapter), into Wenders's "road trilogy"; the retrospective postulation of this trilogy by critics is slightly misleading, though, since Wenders denies that he made the films with this plan in mind. Nevertheless, it is hard to ignore the resemblances that link the works together, anchored by their employment of the same actor in the role of a central protagonist: Rüdiger Vogler. Specifically, like *Alice*, *Kings of the Road* follows two main characters as they drive across Germany, in this case, a stretch between Lüneburg and Hof near the then-border separating West and East Germany. Although the countryside is much less populated than that in *Alice* and the camera captures fewer incidents along this road, *Kings* returns again and again to footage of their van moving through an expansive landscape, bringing to mind *Alice*'s closing shot of the train.

The truck driver and owner is Bruno, a movie projector repairman who services small-town theaters in this area. He has been driving up and down his route for the past couple of years, living alone in his vehicle. He is quite proud of and guarded about his solitude. While he seems to be managing so far, it is clear that business is drying up as the theaters go under.

Into Bruno's life one morning crashes Robert. We first see Robert in a car trailing a cloud of dust across the placid countryside; as he drives, in a shot that alludes to *Alice*, he tears up a photo of his home (Figure 2.1). The road he is following leads right up to the Elbe River and recklessly he speeds into the water. This accident is witnessed by Bruno, who watches Robert swim ashore. When he sees how traumatized Robert is, he laconically offers him some clothes to change into and a ride to the next town.

So begins their journey. Robert, who has just separated from his spouse, gradually responds to Bruno's solicitude and to the break from it all that riding with him represents. Although he makes repeated, if rather half-hearted,

Figure 2.1 *Kings of the Road* directed by Wim Wenders © Wim Wenders Produktion, Munich 1976. All rights reserved.

attempts to call his wife, he starts to let on in small ways that he would not mind traveling with Bruno for a bit longer. As for the latter, although he is somewhat wary of Robert and dislikes the fact that he enjoys as a vacation the travel that for him is a job, he nevertheless ends up inviting Robert to accompany him. It appears that underneath Bruno's solitude is a bit of loneliness after all.

Bruno and Robert's trip together is thus something different from either lost wandering or a focused quest. It is characterized less by the absence or presence of a specific destination and more by the distended course of time, emphasized by the film's German title, that eventually turns them into friends. As in *Alice*, but perhaps to an even more weighted degree, the sheer passing of moment to moment along the road is heightened by the film's episodic form, as the characters stop in one village and then, after a while, in another. This relaxed pace notwithstanding, tensions between them start to mount. Bruno resents the self-consciousness Robert imposes on him and the influence he exercises. Robert feels defensive that his company is not entirely welcome. Their time together seems to be coming to an end.

Four more episodes, though, bind them to each other. The first is their encounter one night with a distraught man who has just lost his wife in an automobile accident. This death-struck griever shakes them up and turns their thoughts to their lives as a whole. The next morning, Robert decides to take a hitchhiking trip on the side to visit his father, which opens the second episode. He spends that next night struggling to communicate to the old man how demoralized he was as a child by the latter's abuse of his mother. As this is occurring, a third, concurrent episode involving Bruno takes place. He drives to the next town on his itinerary, strikes up a conversation with a woman, Pauline, and meets her later at a movie theater where she works as a ticket seller. The theater is showing a piece of pornography; after the screening, he playfully splices together images of destruction, rape, and sex to show her. Watching this clip appears to freeze them, each in his or her solitude, however, and they end up spending the night in the theater apart, unable to approach each other any closer. After Bruno drives away the next day, he picks up Robert at his father's place and they decide to embark on another side trip that forms the fourth episode: a visit to Bruno's old home on an island in the Rhine where he lived alone with his mother. Arriving at the abandoned house after dark, Bruno is deeply moved by the ruin and begins to weep. The following morning—in a scene that recalls a similar one in Nicholas Ray's *The Lusty Men* (1952)—he finds a can under some stairs in which he had stashed some comic books as a child. Some days later, in a moment of closeness to Robert, he tells him: "I'm glad we went to the Rhine. For the first time, I see myself as someone who's gone through a certain time, and that time is my story."

Each of these episodes touches a serious longing in Robert and Bruno; their friendship is sealed as they share these experiences on the road. Robert starts to emerge more clearly as a man who fears he is bound to repeat his father's mistakes with women. For his part, Bruno appears to be running away from the devastating loss of his mother; it figures he would never want to relive that loss with any other woman. These two men connect, then, over their guardedness about the opposite sex. But, of course, what makes women seem so threatening is precisely Bruno and Robert's intense need for the intimacy they hold out that transcends and puts in the pale ordinary friendship. Hence this wariness is bound to be an unstable basis for the two men's bond.

It is no surprise, then, that everything explodes one night they spend together at an abandoned guardhouse on the border. A bottle of whiskey loosens their tongues. Bruno insists that the reason Robert keeps trying to telephone his wife is not that he is worried about her, as he professes, but that he is afraid for himself. Robert lashes back by ridiculing Bruno's dead life of routine inside a moving van-shell. Their fight flares into fisticuffs and after wounding each other, they retreat to separate sides of the room and talk helplessly about their loneliness. It seems neither of them is capable of crossing the line between them to claim the intimacy that they are looking for in women. So the next morning, Robert departs.

Before he does, though, he writes Bruno a note. "Everything must change." The last we see of Robert is that he is on a train, like Alice and Phillip in the earlier film, bound for an unknown destination. As for Bruno, he services one last theater that has already closed because the owner cannot stand to show films "where people stagger out stunned and rigid with stupidity, films that kill any joy of life inside them and destroy any feeling for themselves and the world." At the end of his visit, he climbs back into the van and, as Robert did with his photo of home, rips up his itinerary.

The film ends with each protagonist heading off in different directions. Before they completely separate, however, we see them together in one summative, extraordinarily staged scene. As I mentioned above, Robert is riding in a train; some meters away but directly alongside him, driving on a parallel road, is Bruno, singing along to Roger Miller's single, "King of the Road." For some time, both are synchronous traveling companions. Eventually, their paths cross and turn away from each other; at that juncture, though, each says something to the other in his head. We are thus left with the suggestion that their conversation continues internally even as they move physically apart.

Underneath its wayward course of events, then, *Kings* addresses in a sustained way a concern that is at the center of *Alice* as well: the chasm between people. Bruno and Robert resemble their precursor, Phillip, in being solitary men who find it difficult to live in relationships with others, especially women. More than in the earlier film, though, Wenders traces this problem to the distorting ways that women are seen by men. This is where his previous concern with media images comes back into play. The world of porn flicks and ubiquitous pinups that Bruno lives in makes it, ironically, next to impossible for him to get close to Pauline, who sits walled in in her ticket booth (Figure 2.2). Contrasting what is shown so exploitatively in these works to his own images of time passing naturally between people, Wenders expresses once again a desire for alternative cinematic images that would imply and cultivate a more respectful attitude toward the world's naked appearing.

With its focus on how men struggle with intimacy, *Kings* also takes more of an interest than the earlier film in the role that psychological currents and contradictions play in shaping our lives. Robert is mad at, and fears the perpetuating power of, his father. Bruno longs for, and fears another loss like

Figure 2.2 *Kings of the Road* directed by Wim Wenders © Wim Wenders Produktion, Munich 1976. All rights reserved.

that of, his mother. Although, as in *Alice*, it is road conversation that brings Bruno and Robert together, before aggressively defensive words tear them apart, these men are in addition haunted by their family histories, which spur and fuel their talk.

This more psycho-historical dimension to their lives alters somewhat what destiny means to them. It is no longer, as it was in Phillip's case in *Alice*, a move to authorship from storylessness. Robert, who at one point declares, "I am my story," is already saddled with his father's story; Bruno carries the story of the time he lived through and lost. Destiny, then, is the realization that everything as a whole must change, above all, these histories. At the station where Robert catches his final train out, he acquires from a boy a writing book that the boy shows can effortlessly record the world; when we last see Robert on the train, he appears ready to compose a new, film-like story of his experience of growing out of his old story. And, of course, Bruno's final gesture liberates him from the grip of the course of the past two years. Having spent them driving around, he is now ready to get back really on the road. The destiny to which the road of *Kings* conducts its travelers, then, is that moment when they set forth on rewriting their lives.

In *Kings of the Road*, then, who is being led out? It is two men who are each fleeing their histories. Robert does not want to be his father. Bruno does not want to miss his mother.

From where are they being led? They are drawn away from their fears of being fatally trapped.

To where are they being led? To active, revisionary authorship.

Who or what leads them out? It is the course of time, that is, the road they converse in and share together.

* * *

After four more feature films in eight years, Wenders came out with *Paris, Texas* in 1984. It departs sharply from *Alice* and *Kings*, not only in its setting but also in its narrative form. Its road runs from Devil's Graveyard in Texas to Los Angeles, and then back to places in the Houston area. As the film follows its characters on this journey, it eschews the meandering, episodic form of the earlier works. Instead, it straightforwardly unrolls an unbroken, linear story, un-self-consciously and without ambivalence.

At its center is the man in the opening scene. Dressed in a cheap suit worn to its last threads, he stands alone in the middle of a landscape of desert canyons stretching to the horizon. As a buzzard watches him, he takes a last drink of water and flings the bottle away. He begins to walk deeper into the vast emptiness as a bottleneck guitar twangs some dirge-like notes on the soundtrack (Figure 2.3).

Figure 2.3 *Paris, Texas* directed by Wim Wenders © Road Movies Filmproduktion, Berlin/Argos Film, Paris 1984. All rights reserved.

The setting, the buzzard, and the guitar: these signal that we are in the country of the Western. As the lone man determinedly and fearlessly makes his way in this desert, as if he were on some kind of mission, our questions about him are bound to have mythic overtones. Not only are we intrigued by who this person is, how he came to this place, and where he is going. We may also expect that the answers will shed light on elementary features of our human condition. It appears that the film may be less interested in probing the details of a particular life and more in transparently making up a story that draws attention to these basic facts. Moreover, it will do this by alluding to and revising our common sense of the cowboy hero. John Ford, indeed, lives on.

Right after this opening, *Paris, Texas*'s hero, Travis, collapses at a gas station. A doctor who helps him recover tracks down his brother Walt on the phone, in Los Angeles. Walt flies to a Texas clinic in Terlingua to fetch Travis, but once he arrives he discovers that Travis has fled. He manages to find Travis on the road, but their reunion is tense. Travis is completely mute; he dimly recognizes Walt but does not greet or utter a word to him and several times he tries to escape from Walt back into the inhospitable land. "There's nothing out there!" points out Walt when he catches him for the last time. Finally, Travis allows himself to be coaxed back into Walt's car and they begin their journey back to Walt's home.

This road, then, is one of rescue and return from some mysterious catastrophe. On it, Travis eventually resumes speaking and in dialogue with his brother, he begins to remember things from their family past. He even recalls that he has on him a photo of a lot in Paris, Texas; according to their mother, this is the town in which he was conceived. He refuses to say a word, though, about how he ended up in the wilderness. On his end, Walt gradually begins to inform Travis about some of the things that have happened since the latter disappeared four years ago. In particular, he breaks it to him that Hunter, the son that Travis had with his wife Jane, is now living with him and his French (Parisian?) wife, Anne. Since Hunter was only three when he was left with Walt and Anne by a stranger—Jane had also vanished—he may not even remember Travis. In effect, Walt and Anne have adopted Hunter. As the brothers' conversation develops along this long trip and its course of time—at one point, Walt tries to shorten it by taking a plane but Travis refuses to leave the ground—the passing countryside grows greener and more cultivated and populated. Travis is being reintroduced to language, family, and history.

In Los Angeles, the road travel temporarily comes to a halt, but Travis's journey continues and takes a new turn. Hunter at first refuses to recognize Travis as his father, but when they and Walt and Anne together watch an old home movie, Hunter drops his resistance and embraces Travis. The latter begins to tell Hunter about their family history, although Travis winces at any mention of Jane and there remain gaps in his memory. Over the next few days, Anne watches father and son bond and worries that Travis is going to take the boy away from her. She discloses to Travis that on the same day each month, Jane deposits money for Hunter at a bank in Houston. As Anne hopes, Travis decides to leave LA; he buys a used car to go off in search of Jane. When he tells Hunter his plan, however, Hunter asks to go along; he wants to find his mother. His desire echoes Alice's in the earlier film. Tragically, then, Anne's scheme backfires.

The road that returns Travis to Texas is also where he and Hunter grow closer and he becomes again a full-fledged father, as Phillip did to Alice over their journey together. Correspondingly, the absent Jane grows into a more and more palpable presence. Sure enough, then, at the Houston bank they spot her and they follow her as she drives from there to her job. It turns out that Jane is working in a seedy peep show.

Travis has two lengthy, cathartic dialogues with Jane at this dramatically staged place. In both, he sits in a dark booth and she flounces about in a bright, cheap simulacrum of an ordinary setting, such as a coffee shop or a hotel room. Her confinement in this space recalls Pauline's in the porn-theater ticket booth. As Travis and Jane talk to each other, only he can view her from behind a one-way mirror; she can only see herself. Her job, evidently, is to entertain men by acting out what they tell her they want to watch.

In his first talk with Jane, Travis does not identify himself. The scene begins with him looking deep into himself as he listens intently to the phone; when the camera finally turns to her, it is as if she is an image he has dredged up from the past. He goes from being moved to see her after their long separation, to being touched by her sad predicament, to jealous rage at her availability to other men. He struggles with the contradiction of being both a customer like any other and the man who recognizes the mother of his child. When he realizes that he has become too upset, he breaks off their conversation and flees.

After driving away with Hunter, he makes a beeline for a bar. Standing at the counter with his son and getting more and more drunk, he shows

Hunter his photo of Paris, Texas, and explains that he had hoped to build a house on the empty lot for the three of them to live in as a family. Again, it is hard to mistake the echoes of other home photos in Wenders's earlier films. Hunter shows little interest, though, and expresses more concern about his drinking; Travis then flicks the photo off the counter to the ground. Sometime later, after the fall of dark, Hunter helps him stagger to an all-night laundromat where they can catch some sleep. Before he passes out, though, he tells Hunter this time about how his own father became obsessed with the delusion, which embarrassed his mother, that she was a fancy woman from Paris. And not a plain one from Texas. Travis thus appears to be a cousin of Robert in *Kings*: a man who has inherited his father's sins against his mother. Paris, Texas, emblematizes the contradictory divide that this male attitude has imposed on women from generation to generation. At the nadir of his stupor, speaking to his son from a couch that resembles an analyst's, Travis realizes this.

The next day, after being prodded by Hunter to see Jane again, Travis drops him off at a Houston hotel. At the limits of what he is capable of saying to his child, he leaves him with a tape recording explaining that because it was he who caused Hunter and his mother to be sundered, it is his responsibility to bring them together again. Once he has accomplished that, however, he will not be able to stay with them. He does not believe he can heal the wounds he and Jane have inflicted on each other. He remains attracted to the desert and afraid of where that attraction will lead him; he needs to confront and come to an understanding of that desire and fear alone. An unspoken suggestion left in the air is that he is motivated to conquer his demons and get his act together so that he can act as a father to Hunter, even if from a distance.

Travis returns to the peep show for the second dialogue with Jane. Still concealing his identity, he tells her a story about a woman and a man who were in love. Everything they did together was an adventure. Over time, though, the man became more clinging, more possessive, and more prone to imagine that she was unfaithful; on top of it all, he began to drink. His behavior softened when she became pregnant but after the child was born, she became increasingly irritated by her burden of childcare and longed for release. In response, he drank harder and turned violent, devising ways to confine her physically to the house. One night, he dreamed of being lost in a vast country beyond language where no one knew him. When he awoke, he, along with the whole home, was on fire. His family had fled, and he too kept on running, away from human habitation.

From this confession, Jane recognizes Travis. He then communicates to her the location of Hunter and insists that Hunter needs her. Perhaps the reason he believes this is that he has realized what his real, Texan mother means to him. Jane assures him that she will be there; she silently also appears to agree that she and Travis for now cannot live together. After Travis departs, he watches the reunion of Jane and Hunter in the hotel room from a parking lot across the street—a different kind of peep show. He then gets back in his car and drives off into the last of the sunset.

So who is the man in the film's opening scene, looking like a hero in a Western? It turns out that he is running away from his family that he—not some Indians—destroyed. What draws him into the wilderness is the promise not of adventure but of solace in the wordless, storyless, selfless eternal present. The film's road, in contrast, leads him back to that family and the history he is still involved in. Hunter incarnates his responsibility for this story. When Travis reacknowledges his parenthood, he accepts and affirms this responsibility, which includes seeing that Hunter is not deprived of his mother. This moral desire is what leads him further to confess his story to Jane. At the same time, he realizes that he has been too scarred by their breakup to live with her; he needs to come to terms with the aloneness it has left him with. The film's conclusion is thus quite equivocal and its road open-ended: for all that Travis has come to appreciate his family ties, it is not clear that he can truly be a father to Hunter, or that he will not deny those ties again in the future. Once Travis has told his story, it puts him in the position of being able to live it forward only one struggling step at a time. Anything like a heroic and happy ending has vanished from this revised myth.

Indeed, its Achilles heel turns out to be the male gaze. As we saw, Wenders examined this theme in *Kings*, but here he bears down on it in an especially charged way with the peep-show scenes. Not only do its images dehumanize women and make it difficult for men to enter into intimate relationships with them, but they furthermore corrupt the nuclear family and pass on their stunting effects to boys. The commercially manipulative images that *Alice* criticized have here become an intergenerational assault against our mothers. Now it must be said that in staging these scenes so compellingly, surrounding an attractive star, Nastassja Kinksi, with such suggestive lines, Wenders thoroughly implicates himself in this visual violence he reproduces, as well as all men who can identify with its viewpoint. The difficult-to-watch scenes challenge men to respond with either defiant denial or complicit guilt. They constitute the few moments when this film, which for the most part is more conventional than its predecessors, particularly in its dramatic pacing, takes a self-consciously counter-cinematic turn.

In spite of all this, the film also suggests how these images can be somewhat recoded. At one point in their first meeting, Jane offers to take off her top and Travis stops her; he insists that he just wants to talk. After wandering in the wordless void and then journeying back into conversation with his brother and his son, he is at last ready to tackle an even bigger communicative challenge: turning the peep show into a confessional. It is an ingenious visual conceit. In the role of priest, Jane listens from behind the fantasy that has eclipsed and shrouded her. And Travis, addressing her in his darkness, admitting that what he sees of her is his fault, opens up a passage of honesty around the image. His confession makes it possible for Jane to express the longing behind her listening, one for a true conversation between them (Figure 2.4). Now whether this conversation has a future remains very much in doubt. But in this strange, ambiguous setting, the wonder is that it took place at all.

Figure 2.4 *Paris, Texas* directed by Wim Wenders © Road Movies Filmproduktion, Berlin/Argos Film, Paris 1984. All rights reserved.

In *Paris, Texas*, who is being led out? It is Travis, a man who is fleeing what he did to his family and who is lost in the wilderness, nearing death.

From where is he being led? From his self-centered hunger for oblivion.

To where is he being led? To taking moral responsibility for healing his family and talking to the woman he loves.

Who or what is leading him out? It is his son Hunter, who needs a real mother and not a sexy image.

* * *

Even in its making, *Until the End of the World* represents an odyssey. Conceived in 1977, the picture was finally released in 1991, but merely in what Wenders now calls a "Reader's Digest version"; the director's complete, almost five-hour cut saw the light of day only in 2015.[3] This film too breaks strikingly new ground. It is a science-fiction story, set in the then-near future of 1999. It is also an old-fashioned love story, although the central couple is surrounded by a host of secondary characters; in the end, it also twists into a rather unexpected friendship story. Along with its exotic costumes and décor, it employs elements that we have not seen much of until now, such as suspenseful chases, preposterous pratfalls, and campy wisecracks; its drama is very much leavened by humor. Perhaps what sets it off most from the earlier works is that its central protagonist is a young woman, Claire. In the course of the film, she travels from Venice to Paris, to Berlin, to Lisbon, to Moscow, to Beijing, to Tokyo, to San Francisco, and to Australia's outback, ending with her on an orbiting space station. Her road encompasses the whole globe.

In this spirit, the film opens in the midst of a planetary crisis. A nuclear satellite is falling out of orbit; the US military, over the objections of others, is preparing to shoot it down, heedless of the possible chain reaction explosions this might set off. In the meantime, Claire, who has separated from her boyfriend, Gene, over an infidelity of his, is wandering around Venice. For his part, remorseful Gene has retreated into a solitary life in their Paris apartment, praying that she will return. As he waits, he begins to compose a novel about her; it forms the film's overarching voiceover narration. It starts: "For two

---

[3] Wenders has used this phrase repeatedly in relating the genesis of the film. See, for example, Peter Keough, "Fuse Film Interview: Until the End of the Movies—Wim Wenders on His New Retrospective," *The Arts Fuse*, December 10, 2015, artsfuse.org/138381/fuse-film-interview-until-the-end-of-the-movies-wim-wenders-on-his-new-retrospective.

months, Claire had drifted through the parties, designer drugs, and one-night stands, seeking excuses to obliterate herself. Until she realized that if she was to go on living, she couldn't go on living like this." *La Serenissima* has been for her akin to Travis's Devil's Graveyard.

Departing it for home, like Phillip in *Alice*, then, disenchanted Claire is driving along when she suddenly collides with another auto. This triggers an epiphany in her. Gene recounts it as follows:

> Claire felt strangely light. She knew she had been meant to die here, on the plateau of Lazaire. It was a miracle she was alive. The angels had somehow made a mistake in their accounting and had left her a precious gift. She had been given a whole new life which she could use this time to be a better person. She could be of service. All she needed was an opportunity, a mission.

The occupants of the other vehicle, who also survived the crash, are a couple of bank robbers on the lam. She befriends them and agrees to transport the money for safekeeping in her flat in exchange for a third of the heist. Stopping along the way to have her car windshield repaired, she encounters a man who introduces himself as Trevor, whom, she notices, is being tailed by another man, Burt. On the spur of the moment, she springs Trevor from Burt's clutches and the two of them hightail it together to Paris. After Trevor warmly takes leave of her and after she stiffly returns Gene's greetings at their apartment, she tells Gene about her deal with the robbers. But when she shows him the money, she discovers that she has been robbed in turn by Trevor. So much for her first attempt at being of service.

On a subsequent day, Claire notices Burt at a metro stop. She impulsively follows him and overhears him telling someone on the phone that Trevor is at an address in Berlin. She decides to go to him there. Although she claims it is her money that she wants back from him, Gene suspects that she is "in love with the idea of being in love" and is chasing a projection of her imagination. In any case, her road now turns into one of pursuit. Trevor incarnates what her postaccident epiphany prophesized.

When Claire succeeds in getting to Trevor before Burt does, she rather comically warns him, "You're being followed!" Trevor keeps eluding both of them, though, hopping from city to city; at each run-in with her, he takes more of her money. For help, she hires a private detective, Phillip Winter—*Alice's* protagonist has evidently changed professions!—and eventually she is also joined in the chase by Gene, who is trying to reingratiate himself with her while suppressing his jealousy. After the four of them, to various degrees farcically competing with each other, narrowly miss catching Trevor a few times, she finally comes upon him defenseless in a Tokyo pachinko parlor. As Gene puts it: "All Claire knew was that she had finally found her mission. The man she loved was almost blind and needed her." He had stolen her completely.

Crippled by an eye affliction, Trevor lets himself be led by Claire; she takes him on a train out of Tokyo and they get off haphazardly at Hakone. It turns out that the man running a local inn is a herbal doctor; his medicine and her care succeed in restoring Trevor's sight. Trevor now trusts and loves Claire; he discloses to her that his real name is Sam Farber and that he is being hunted because he has stolen back from the US government a device invented by his father. This machine enables blind people to see the images its operator records by registering and combining both what the observer sees and what he or she feels about what is seen. (In a sense, Wenders has invented here an interpretation of the concept of "moving pictures.") Unfortunately, operating the device puts such a strain on the eyes that Sam almost turns into one of those blind people himself. In any event, he has separated himself from his own wife and child in order to collect images of family members to present to his sightless mother. He has one more shooting to do of his sister in San Francisco.

Claire accompanies him there; unlike the traveling pairs in the previous films, they have become an outlaw couple like Bonny and Clyde. In fact, it turns out that she has better eyes for recording these images than Sam does. Once again, though, this work is harried by pursuers. Unlike the meandering and relaxing roads of *Alice* and *Kings*, or even the road of remembrance in *Paris*, this one hurries its travelers forward and narrows their attention to the prize they crave. Furthermore, in the style of *Paris*, Claire's hunt for Trevor and then her getaway with Sam makes for a continuous story, although the different cities do give that story a residual episodic coloring. At any rate, following another close call, they are rescued by one of her bank-robber friends, Chico, and they make their way to Australia where they are, in addition, assisted by Sam's friend, David. After further scrapes and escapes, in which the fast pace of events is given an extra snap by the growing cast of characters the viewer has to keep track of, the couple and its entourage is united when the nuclear satellite is shot down and the blast disrupts all the power in the region. The whole, abruptly stranded, band of travelers joins a caravan of people fleeing radiation into the outback; they make their way to a remote science station in Aborigine country presided over by Sam's father, Henry, and his mother, Edith. All that road travel leads finally to a family reunion in a laboratory in a cave.

At this point, the story slows down. Most of the people around the outpost spend the following months worrying about whether the rest of the world has survived the satellite blast, since all long-distance communication has been terminated. While they wait in stasis for some sign of the earth's fate to appear, Gene types away at his novel and Phillip, Chico, Burt, David, and others bring into being a new kind of music. The Farbers and Claire, however, forget all about the possible apocalypse in their preoccupation with their science project. After a number of failed attempts that expose the friction between father and son, Henry and Sam, with Claire's pivotal help, at last succeed in transmitting the recorded images to Edith. At first, she is overjoyed. But gradually, she becomes disillusioned and disgusted that the world is not what she had imagined. She loses her will to live and passes away.

At the same time as Edith's death, the group discovers that the world still lives. Phillip, Chico, Burt, and others depart from the compound; Gene stays and continues his writing. After a too-brief period of mourning, Claire, Sam, and Henry become even more obsessed with a new project to capture images of dreams. Soon, they become addicted to their own dream images and lose their connections to each other and anyone else; their Aborigine friends are repulsed by this and desert them. At the nadir of their fall into narcissism, Henry is captured by American soldiers and brought back to the United States. Sam is brought out of his condition by David who leads him on a walkabout through the calming countryside; Sam eventually finds his way back to the States only to discover that his father has died and that his wife and child have moved on without him. And after a protracted, painful struggle with image withdrawal, Claire is delivered by Gene who, keeping her company while finishing the novel, at last gives her her story to read. Claire and Gene no longer desire to live together as a couple but they cement their friendship. Sometime later, he calls her at her new workplace on a space station that monitors the earth for pollution crimes; he shares the news that his novel, *Dance around the Planet*, has been published and wishes her a happy birthday. In the end, she has devoted her keen vision to the planet's health.

Claire's story, then, like that of Phillip's in *Alice*, is about being lost and then being found. At first, she believed that she had found her own way out of her wandering in Sam; pursuing, rescuing, assisting, and loving him became her mission. But his mission involved them with mad-science, double-edged image technologies. On the one hand, these technologies enable the blind to see their loved ones; on the other, their images overpower and devalue our imagination. On the one hand, they enable us to see our dreams; on the other, they hook us to ourselves and destroy our relationships. Sam, the man who was trying to gather together images of his relatives for the benefit of his mother, a man who nevertheless lived in characteristically Wendersian fashion in tension with his father, ended up tragically losing all of his family, including Claire. And she lost her passion for him; while Gene, having watched and suffered that passion and her withdrawal into herself, lost his need for her. Accordingly, Wenders's indictment of our image world has broadened to target not only its manipulative and sexist assault on us, but also the way it infects us with narcissism (Figure 2.5). He suggests that when our desire for a sense of purpose falls prey to an infatuation with a mere image, it is bound to turn into something more self-centered.

Nevertheless, Claire is, indeed, found by the healing grace of Gene's story. Its words transform her experiences from dream-like, disjunctive, intensely

Figure 2.5 *Until the End of the World* directed by Wim Wenders © Road Movies Filmproduktion, Berlin/Argos Film, Paris/Village Roadshow Pictures 1991. All rights reserved.

private moments to be repetitively re-savored and nostalgically possessed, like those Phillip hoped to capture in his American photographs in *Alice*, back into a unifying and continuing chain of responses to others and to the common world, one that is forged from the perspective of someone who is linked to and loves her. Gene's narrative saves her from a *Paris, Texas*-like wasteland of images. It connects her and him to the earth and gives them a stake in its peaceful health (Figure 2.6). At last, she is placed in the grip of a larger mission and in a relationship that supports it. As I noted earlier, what starts out as a love story about one couple morphs into a friendship story about another.

Now it is true that Claire is not the author of this tale but its reader; the story is one of the things that happen to her. How, then, can it constitute her destiny, particularly since I have been emphasizing that destiny is an act of invention? The answer, I think, is that it actually does more than that: the story constitutes Claire *and* Gene's destiny. After all, he places himself in the story as well; as he tells it, it is their relationship and interactions, their up and down conversation among and about the new people that appear in their lives, that produces the story. Thus in a more precise sense, both its authorship and its readership are collective, as is the sense of direction it broaches. This understanding that our destinies grow out of, and cannot help but bear witness to, our joint participation in the world's life is what I find to be one of *Until*

Figure 2.6 *Until the End of the World* directed by Wim Wenders © Road Movies Filmproduktion, Berlin/Argos Film, Paris/Village Roadshow Pictures 1991. All rights reserved.

the End of the World's most innovative insights. It is elaborated in some of Wenders's subsequent films.

Who in this film is being led out? It is Claire, who wants a mission for her spared life. And Gene, who wants Claire to return and restore his past life.

From where are they being led? Claire is drawn away first from her wandering in self-oblivion and then from her self-centered infatuation. And Gene is drawn away from his possessiveness as he follows and accompanies her.

To where are they being led? They are drawn to a renewal of their friendship based on their true missions: his as a novelist and hers as an environmentalist.

What leads them out? The story they both ultimately author, one about, and to, both of them. At its center is Sam and his tragic preoccupation with technologically produced images.

* * *

The last two films I shall examine in this chapter were made much later in Wenders's career, after he had completed seven additional features in other genres. (In Chapter 5, though, I shall argue that at least one of the latter can be understood to be a figurative road movie.) It would be fair to call both films only quasi- or partial road movies, because the centrality of their road journeys to their stories is open to dispute. Nevertheless, I include them because I interpret these stories to be figurative extensions of these journeys that the films do depict, however brief the footage of the latter is. In this way, the works represent a transition to the kind of movies in which the road is entirely metaphorical and literally disappears.

Land of Plenty came out in 2004. It is unlike any previous film of Wenders in that it is forthrightly political: it responds to the reactionary turn in the United States following 9/11. The story concerns the meeting and bonding of two protagonists: Paul, a Vietnam veteran, and his niece Lana, a Christian missionary. We could say that the film explores how a better union of patriotism and religion might develop. Paul is rooted in Los Angeles; Lana flies back to that city from Palestine, where she has been living and working with her father. As the film approaches its denouement, they drive together from the metropolis to the small, desolate town of Trona, California, and from there they set out on a cross-country trip to New York City.

Paul is on an unending, vigilante mission to protect LA from jihadists. He works nonstop at his own initiative, fueled by love of country and hatred for those who attacked it. He is loyally assisted by a Sancho Panza-like character who was formerly under his command, Jimmy. Daily and in solitude, Paul patrols the city, employing video surveillance equipment to look for anything out of the ordinary that might signal a terrorist threat. Some of the shots of street life resemble those in *Alice*, only here they are framed by Paul's paranoid point of view. As he drives around, he listens continuously to conservative talk radio. Besides being contemptuous of those who disagree with his politics, he is humorless, hot-tempered, a heavy drinker, and not very quick; he is right on the edge of being a right-wing nut. But Wenders gives him other traits that humanize him—and that prevent the filmmaker from lapsing into left-wing caricature. Paul is struggling with regular attacks of pain following his exposure to Agent Pink in Vietnam. And it turns out that he and Jimmy were the only survivors after their helicopter was shot down in that war; he still has devastating nightmares about that event. It is hard to be unmoved by his enduring devotion, in the teeth of this personal misery, to a larger cause.

After landing in Los Angeles, Lana takes up work at a mission that serves the homeless. The shelter is run by a pastor named Henry; when he meets her at the airport and drives her to her new home, we learn from their conversation that she had insisted, over her father's objections, on coming back to the States. In effect, she feels called to her home country. She is strikingly devout; she regularly prays to God for strength and guidance and thanks God for every moment of her life.

Initially, the film introduces us in an episodic way to the separate image worlds of Lana and Paul. As she looks at the city, she is concerned by the blocks and blocks of people sleeping on the street. As he looks at it, he is concerned by an unguarded airport full of planes that could be used as weapons.

The story begins when Lana, holding a typically Wendersian photo of herself as a child with Uncle Paul, embarks on an *Alice*-like quest to find him. She wants to deliver a letter from her deceased mother who had become estranged from her brother. She shows up at his house and manages to get Jimmy, who denies Paul lives there, to, nevertheless, give her Paul's cellphone number. Ever cautious, Paul refuses to take her call but does return it from a pay phone. Although he does not divulge his name when he speaks to her, she recognizes his voice. He, though, refuses to confirm his identity or admit that he knows her.

In the meantime, Paul's roving and suspicious eye is caught by an Arab-looking man on the street talking with another and acquiring from him a box of Borax. ("To make a clean bomb," Jimmy quips, before a look brings him back to the work.) At first, Paul loses the trail of this potential terrorist, but when he visits the mission to scope out Lana in secret, he catches sight of the man again. This fellow introduces himself to Lana in the food line as Hassan and responds to her query about where he is from by declaring: "My home is not a place. It is people."

When Hassan leaves the shelter, Paul tails him. At this point, Lana is searching for Paul and Paul is following Hassan, looking for the cell to which he presumably belongs. One evening, Paul stakes out Hassan as the latter prepares to camp with other homeless outside the mission. Suddenly, someone drives by and shoots Hassan. Paul, Lana, Henry, and others rush to him and as he dies, a dazed Paul turns to the stricken Lana and tells her that she looks just like her mother.

Paul becomes obsessed with cracking the case of Hassan's assassination and the larger forces at work in it. Lana, on the other hand, wants to locate Hassan's kin. She discovers from the police that he has a brother, Youssef, in Trona. She ingratiates herself with her difficult uncle by sharing this information and persuades Paul that it would give him an opportunity to gather more if he and she were to transport Hassan's body to Youssef for burial.

Brought together by the death of Hassan, a man who is both penniless and terrorist-looking, then, niece and uncle set off on the road to Trona. Paul asserts to Lana that he is not some crazy vet and that the true story of the Vietnam War is that the United States won. Lana asks him why he never answered her mother's letters. Vaguely, he tries to explain that he felt called to break away from his old life. Their awkward conversation hits an especially tense point when Lana brings up "everything America is *supposed* to stand for."

After Paul drops Lana off at Youssef's trailer park, she and Youssef bond over old family photos. Meanwhile, Paul deposits the body at the funeral parlor and then spots and chases who he believes are the terrorists he has been searching for. As he singlehandedly prepares to confront them, he tells himself, "These are the moments that define your life." But they turn out to be movers who are simply using Borax boxes to pack up an old lady's household.

Paul's imagined conspiracy collapses. Jimmy calls with the news that Hassan was murdered on a whim by some kids on drugs. When Paul returns to Lana, he and she hear anecdotes from Youssef about what a gentle and winning person Hassan was. Paul feels his whole world giving way. Later, while dead drunk in a motel room, he dreams again of himself in his helicopter falling from the sky.

The next day, conversing with Lana at the graveyard, Paul likens his nightmare to the image of the Twin Towers being unable to remain standing proud and strong after being attacked. He is haunted by American vulnerability and weakness. Lana explains that her nightmare is that something has gone terribly wrong with the country, because she watched ordinary Palestinians cheering the towers' fall. She is haunted by American corruption.

Lana pleads with Paul that they need to listen to the voices of the innocent victims of the 9/11 disaster who would not want others to be killed in their name, like Hassan. She gives Paul her mother's letter, written on her deathbed, which asks him to help Lana develop courage; the mother concludes, in a voiceover as they drive away, by enjoining her brother to watch over his niece while she watches over them both. This letter suggests that the absent mother, a central figure in *Alice*, *Kings*, and *Paris*, constitutes the overarching point of view of the whole film. Under her felt gaze, they embark on a road trip across the country, captured in a montage of travel footage, which takes them to Ground Zero. There they stand still in silence.

Despite the fact that *Land of Plenty* is politically pointed in a new way for Wenders, we can find in it many of his now-familiar themes. There is the idea of family, to be sure, which is sharpened by our longing for it amid our experiences of isolation and hurt. There is the deceptive nature of images, which can fuel the divisive imagination of conspiracy. There is the healing power of conversation, which gives rise to family feeling. Perhaps the most moving one the film invites us to enter into is that staged by its last shot: a conversation between ourselves and the speechless, Hassan-like victims of violence (Figure 2.7). And there are the stories that give meaning and direction to our lives. Paul is driven by one of military weakness and the need for revenge. Lana has been inspired by the Christian one of moral elevation. Without abandoning these stories, they recognize, like Robert and Bruno in *Kings*, that "everything must change" and that they need to revise them wholly. They start to do so together on the road to the Trona cemetery and then to the gaping wound in NYC.

Who in *Land of Plenty* is being led out? It is Paul, a soldier traumatized by defeat, and Lana, a missionary traumatized by the hate directed at her country

Figure 2.7 *Land of Plenty* directed by Wim Wenders © Reverse Angle/IFC Films/InDigEnt 2004. All rights reserved.

by the people she serves. Both have lost their sense of what it means to be American.

From where are they being led? They are drawn away from their confidence in the stories of American military and moral strength that they had taken for granted.

To where are they being led? They are drawn to an acknowledgment of our shared vulnerability and innocence.

Who or what leads them out? It is their involvement with Hassan, capped by Youssef's stories about him, that raises guiding questions for their lives.

* * *

A year later, in 2005, Wenders released *Don't Come Knocking*. This work represents a second collaboration with Sam Shepard who was the chief writer of *Paris, Texas*; he co-wrote this film and played the leading role. In some ways, the film is a more lighthearted, even farcical retelling of the story of Travis. The men in it in particular are more fools than heroes.

The name of Shepard's character is Howard. We see him open the film on an archetypal, *Paris, Texas*-esque note: dressed as a cowboy, he rides off on horseback into a scrubby and rocky Western landscape. This image is swiftly subverted when the camera pans to the nearby trailer camp of a film crew. It turns out that the star of this picture is fleeing its production team (Figure 2.8).

Figure 2.8 *Don't Come Knocking* directed by Wim Wenders © Reverse Angle/Arte France Cinéma 2005. All rights reserved.

Shortly after his disappearance, a clownish bond man-cum-bounty hunter, Sutter, descends from a helicopter on a mission to fetch Howard back, giving a chase tempo to the story. Howard's journey, with Sutter on his heels, follows the road from the movie location in Moab, Utah, to Elko, Nevada, and then on to Butte, Montana.

Howard is in an existential crisis. The reason he is running away from the celebrity, partying life is that he has come to doubt it has any meaning. In his next scene after his opening one—unfortunately, it has been cut from the shorter, American version of the film—he takes a breather next to a campfire and mutters to himself, "How can I not be dead?" In the original German screenplay, this thought is elaborated further: "I might just as well be dead. It wouldn't make any difference."[4]

After eluding the dragnet out to catch him, Howard drives a rented car to a bus station and catches a bus to visit his mother. She has been absent from his life for the past thirty years and he appears to reflect on this passage of time as he stares out of these vehicles. When he arrives at Elko, rather nervous, his mother welcomes him, despite this long period of incommunicativeness. In town, he is recognized by an old acquaintance, Cliff, but he vehemently rejects the association and their past. Evidently, it was to ditch that past that Howard left town all those years ago in the first place. At any rate, after his

---

[4] Sam Shepard and Wim Wenders, *Don't Come Knocking: Das Buch zum Film* (Berlin: Schwartzkopff Buchwerke, 2005), 19 (my translation).

mother retires for the night, he wanders into a dazzling casino and ends up euphorically gambling away his money, drinking away his self-control, and getting arrested by the police. This has become, more recently, his routine mode of escape.

The next morning, after a cop brings him home, Howard's mother gently scolds him for the previous night and his years of excess and tabloid scandal. With a hangdog face, he replies that he no longer knows what to do with himself. She asks if he has any photos of his family. (What is this, a Wenders film?) Astonished by this request, he learns that a long time ago a woman telephoned his mother and told her she has had his son, without leaving any name. He seems to know who she must be, though, and he decides to travel in his late father's old car to see her. As he does this, a mysterious young woman named Sky, carrying her mother's ashes, is also depicted traveling to Butte. And shortly after his departure, Sutter shows up hot on this trail; he seems to be figuring out that the town is his destination as well.

When Howard arrives there, he is recognized by Sky but he scurries away, treating her like some kind of annoying fan. Then, he recognizes Doreen, the woman he is looking for, and follows her to a music joint. Earl, Doreen's son, is playing there, along with his girlfriend, Amber. Although Doreen is surprised to see Howard, she is cool to him; she simply points out their son and leaves. When Howard follows Earl to the back lot after the music set, Earl, sensing something is up, asks why he is looking at him in the same challenging tone in which Howard had earlier addressed Cliff. Earl and Howard have a heated exchange, which escalates into a near-fight when Howard blurts out that he is his father.

Speeding away from Earl and their failed meeting, Howard heads out of town but then abruptly turns around. The next day, he visits the restaurant where Doreen works and draws her into conversation. He confesses that at first, he wanted to see Earl out of simple curiosity, but was not prepared for the shock of seeing himself in him. Especially, his own fear and lack. That revelatory mirror has brought him back.

Howard visits Earl at his house but he still does not want to have anything to do with him. After Earl, like Howard earlier, storms off, Howard sits motionless on a couch on the street that Earl had heaved out of a window; indifferent to all this drama, traffic goes stolidly by and darkness gradually falls. In the middle of his ruminations, Sky shows up and they start talking. Although he had earlier shooed her away, he is evidently ready this time to recognize her as his daughter from yet another woman he met in Butte; his liaisons took place when he was acting there in the movie *The Return of Jesse James*. Sky explains that Earl is afraid of being related. She asks Howard if he wants to be related and, if so, why he waited so long to show himself. He avows that he does; he worries now that he had missed something and thrown everything away by cutting himself off from his family. As for the time, he simply "didn't know it was passing." She suggests, then, that they make Butte their home; accordingly, she goes off and deposits her mother's ashes on a height overlooking the town.

The next morning, Howard tracks down Doreen. He communicates to her the idea of the two of them settling down together in town. She accuses him of cowardice, though, of running to her, another one of his women, to avoid reaching an understanding with his son, his younger self. In the meantime, Earl admits to Sky, who has approached him as a brother, that he once felt there was something lacking in his life and that he was falling into that void. But he had broken free and never wants to return to that vulnerability. It does seem, indeed, that he is a chip off the old block, not to mention, off many of Wenders's other men in earlier films.

After Howard has arrived at this impasse, he is finally caught up to by Sutter and taken into custody. Howard is able to persuade him, however, to let him say goodbye to his children. Outside Earl's house, in one of the film's most affecting scenes, Sky tells Howard that she is never really sure whether there is something physical linking them; she says this as they unclasp their hands in an image that recalls *The Creation of Adam* by Michelangelo (Figure 2.9).

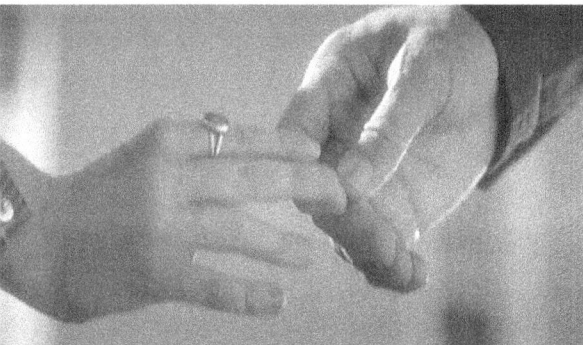

Figure 2.9 *Don't Come Knocking* directed by Wim Wenders © Reverse Angle/Arte France Cinéma 2005. All rights reserved.

The family resemblance among the film's characters is something stubbornly and mysteriously ambiguous, which is precisely what calls them to keep talking about it. On the other hand, Earl at last recognizes the relation. Howard leaves him his father's automobile and Sutter transports his prisoner back to Moab.

Finally back at the movie set with the camera rolling, Howard, once more in costume and on horseback, tells his make-believe gal that he will always keep her in his heart as he rides off into the distance. Meanwhile, Earl, Sky, and Amber are driving together in the old family car on their road into the distance, singing a song about looking for Howard. The film's last shot is of a sign they pass in the hilly, big-sky landscape: "Divide 1 / Wisdom 52."

Like *Paris, Texas*, then, *Don't Come Knocking* is a kind of post-Western. It tells a story about what is behind the myth. Howard begins his journey lost in an isolation of his own doing. In this, he resembles not only Travis, but virtually all the protagonists in the other films we have examined: think too of Phillip, Robert, Bruno, and Paul. (*Until the End of the World* is the qualified exception to this rule: Claire and Sam in the course of the film fall into this isolation; only Gene seems largely spared from it. In *Land of Plenty*, Lana, another of Wenders's few female protagonists, represents the single positive counter-example.) Howard's road is a quest back to history and to family connection, looking for a way in which his life would matter to someone. As in Travis's case, it is not clear that Howard is completely out of the woods at the film's end: Travis is still heading off alone into the unknown at the close of *Paris*; Howard, in a more parodic vein, is doing the same at the finale of his story. But I find a key difference in the later film. It is that Howard's children are coming after him. He has become part of their destinies. In this fashion, Wenders shows how the Western, with its myth of the heroic male individual, may give birth to another, very different kind of shadow story: that of a family of grown-up children riding off to save their lost, cowboy-actor of a father in distress. They are the latter's grace.

Moreover, one could say that the contradictions from which this protagonist suffers are rooted, as we would expect with Wenders, in the world of media images. Howard can maintain the image of a heroic individual only through acting, that is, pretending to be someone he is not. This role draws him into a life not only of dissipation and self-oblivion, but also of loneliness. No matter how many women he hooks up with, he cannot turn such momentary liaisons into a story of relation. Nor can he transform such a cutoff life into one of meaningful purpose.

What sparks the family story that brings the children to the rescue is a different kind of image. It is one that, as Sky observes in her closing speech, is much less tangible and clear. Despite its ineffability, however, it allows us to see the fear and lack we share with others. This is what Sky, Howard, Earl, and even Amber recognize in each other; it is what makes them cousins of Lana and Paul, too, in *Land*. Interestingly, there is even the hint that this image recognition can bring us together when conversation falls apart. Compared to the earlier films, the talk in this one appears much less effective in bonding people. This may also be why, for the first time, there is no story or storyteller that plays an explicit role within the film's story. Admittedly, this makes it more questionable that the latter is about destiny. The reason I think it, nevertheless, is, even if in a more implicit and suggestive way, is that the image of the three young people in the family car, united in their quest for Howard, departs so strikingly from their previous images of unrelatedness. It feels like there must be a story behind that transformation, one, again, that they authored and took in together on the road, one based, comically, on "the return of Jesse James."

In *Don't Come Knocking*, who is being led out? It is Howard, who is fleeing a meaningless life.

From where is he being led? He is drawn away from his need for independence.

To where is he being led? He is drawn to a life of relatedness.

Who or what is leading him out? It is the ways he is recognized and embraced by his family.

***

This chapter has surveyed the other fictional feature films in Wenders's oeuvre, after *Alice in the Cities*, which compose stories about road trips: *Kings of the Road*; *Paris, Texas*; *Until the End of the World*; *Land of Plenty*; and *Don't Come Knocking*. Delving into each in turn, I have explained the different ways in which these stories are, furthermore, about their protagonists' destinies. Even as I attend to what is distinctive about the stories, what also come to light are a handful of common *idées fixes*, themes and concerns that Wenders returns to again and again. Lost isolation, family relation, the consumption of problematic images, bonding conversation, and redemptive stories: out of these building blocks, the same ones featured in *Alice*, he constructs a broad range of variations on the latter's road movie and destiny story. Since, as I mentioned, this chapter strives to respect the singular nature of the films, I have not done much with these conventional elements beyond simply noticing them. In the next chapter, I shall explain how the works made up of them form a coherent mini-genre. I shall also demonstrate that we can arrive at a clearer sense of what this genre stands for by examining how it significantly contrasts with other genres that address some of these same concerns and themes. The Wenders road movie, it turns out, stresses in a particularly distinct fashion their stories' educational meaning.

3

Genre Contrasts

Now that I have examined six films of Wenders that are all about road trips and realizations of destiny, and have remarked on some other ways they resemble each other, it is time to explicate how they form a kind of mini-genre. In addition to articulating the themes and approaches they share, I think it would be helpful for me to place these elements in relation to similar ones in other established genres. Consolidation and contrast, then, are the two main aims of this chapter. The Wenders road movie is a narrative form for making sense of a person's experience of traveling. Indeed, it invites us to understand how one's entire life is like being on the road: this is what I mean by destiny. These travel and destiny stories, moreover, diverge in significant ways from stories in neighboring narrative genres of film and literature. Such differences testify to the pathbreaking and, I have been arguing, philosophical achievement of Wenders's work.

My first task, then, is to sketch out a set of concerns and a line of thinking to which the six Wenders road movie stories are responding, but to do this in a way that evokes the inexhaustible range of variant possibilities that this subgenre encourages us to explore. After I have taken a crack at this, I shall then examine how the concerns that matter most for the genre are taken up in contrasting narrative forms. The most obvious theme of the Wenders road movie is travel. Accordingly, I take a look at how its travel stories differ, on the one hand, from those in more mainstream road movies, including Wenders's own *Lisbon Story*, and on the other, from those in travelogue films. I concentrate in particular on what is widely considered the archetypal road movie, *Easy Rider*, and on Wenders's own quasi-travelogue, *Tokyo-ga*. A second theme I have repeatedly emphasized is that of destiny. In order to distinguish this narrative concept from that of tragic fate, I turn to film noir.

I reflect on *Detour*, a classic in that genre that is also about a road trip, as well as on Wenders's own noir, *The American Friend*. Finally, I have been asserting that the Wenders road movie ultimately offers us a vision not only of being on the road, but also of being led out, another name for education. Most of my argument in support of this claim will be articulated in the next chapter, but as a prelude to it, I examine here how the genre compares with the literary one of the *Bildungsroman*, the novel of formation. My focus is on how Wenders adapts the premier text of the latter, *Wilhelm Meister's Apprenticeship*, into the movie *Wrong Move*. Hopefully, these various comparisons and contrasts will enable us to sharpen our sense of what makes the Wenders road movie such an original and revelatory invention.

* * *

To call a work a road movie is patently to signal that it is about a road or roads, and more specifically, about traveling on them. If we, furthermore, understand that the film conveys a fictional story, we would expect it to have something interesting to show us about this experience. What may travel feel like? Why might it be important?

The Wenders road movie responds to these expectations and questions. It returns constantly, like a song refrain, to footage of people in a vehicle moving across a sizeable landscape; the camera and characters are going somewhere a considerable distance away. Right off the bat, they are *not* stationary. Indeed, such movement in space as well as time is virtually tailor-made for the cinematic medium. This means that the film's opening impressions are of what the traveler or travelers are leaving. Furthermore, because of the priority of this experience of departure, where the travelers are going to is prone to be much less tangible and certain.

The protagonists in this genre, accordingly, begin in a state of flight. They are introduced to us as being on the run; we perceive them traveling away from something they reject or fear even before we understand what that thing is. Also in line with the priority of departure, we grasp that they lack a sense of direction as they enter a strange place. Somewhat lost and afraid, seeking shelter and reassuring familiarity: this is a commencement point shared by the likes of Phillip, Alice, Bruno, Robert, Travis, Claire, Paul, and Lana.

Now as is explicitly indicated in the case of Howard, this apprehensive and wandering condition can stretch over one's life as a whole. Does it make any real difference whether one is alive or dead? Such a question expresses anxiety that one has been wasting one's life. It roots the predicament of the genre's travelers in something that is much larger than some particular problem: death is not anything that can be solved. Driving their journey, then, is on the one hand a need to escape from a place, and specifically a way of life in it that does not feel worth living, and on the other, a dream of an alternative place and life that would somehow make it possible for them to accept, and even affirm, their mortality. Although the existential nature of this flight and quest may be only implicit and not fully understood by those engaged in it, I find that it anchors the central, most powerfully expressive trope of the Wenders road movie: that being on the road, starting with the experience of departure, flight, and lost-ness, is like living a life. This is why even in the midst of feeling abandoned by anything like the embrace of home, the travelers can feel a kind of ecstatic abandon. They are alive! For this reason, too, we discern that in Phillip's struggles with his photography, or Robert's with his father, or Paul's with terrorist plots, what is ultimately at stake is the very meaning of that struggle.

Because this condition of being on the road, of questing for a place different from one's past abode that would reconcile one to one's future demise, is something that is scarcely addressed by our everyday culture, let alone our institutions, it tends to isolate those who are in its grip from others. There is no widely available and approved language for the former to reflect on and discuss this anxiety. It is not surprising, then, that virtually all of Wenders's protagonists are loners. Lacking social support or even intelligibility, they tend to compensate by developing a positive taste for freedom and independence, and a guardedness about losing themselves in others and their experiences in others' words. In particular, they are always ready to move on, whenever, and to wherever, they feel like moving. Such a character thus starts out as a solitary, rootless, rolling stone.

He also tends to be male. Indeed, the two partial exceptions to the loner rule are Claire and Lana, who respond to their aloneness by directly pursuing relationships with others. However touchy this issue, it should be acknowledged that the Wenders road movie has so far been liable to reproduce some gender stereotypes. The opening flight of the main character into unsociability easily slips into some of the familiar dramas of the male psyche; correspondingly, the women viewed from this point of view tend to be objects of ambivalent longing and wariness. Although Wenders has experimented a few times with female protagonists, he seems to have for the most part accepted that his stories especially suit the men of our day. His characteristic way of following through on this point of view is twofold. First, it is to stress in a confessional way that the typically masculine response to the condition of being on the road does violence to women. And second, it is to affirm that the supposedly feminine appreciation of relatedness plays an essential role in the realization of anyone's destiny. In effect, his stories pressure men who identify with them to become more androgynous and less invested in gender division.

Now as we have seen, Wenders traces much of this stereotyping to the distorting power of mass media images. In general, these images and their industries are his films' bad guys. They bear responsibility for producing the poisonous wasteland from which the protagonists are struggling to extricate themselves. Precisely by visualizing the better life that they, like many of us, are longing for, but in crude pictures of desire uninhibitedly and effortlessly satiated, they manage to exploit and manipulate that longing in the service of the status quo. The more we consume and follow the promptings of these images, the less life changes.

In contrast, the Wenders road movie suggests that a more meaningful life calls for a correspondingly different way of viewing the world. His films aspire to cultivate in their viewers a more appreciative and receptive attitude toward the sheer appearing of things and people. Naturally happening life: this is where these films find visual beauty.

At the beginning of these road movies, then, the protagonists are fleeing a place in which they have not just lost something that stands for their innocence, but they are losing their lives. In reaction, they are hoping to find a different place in which they can live less painfully meaningless, more satisfyingly meaningful lives. (I use this somewhat clumsy formulation in order to register the difference in degree between Travis, who is mainly interested in the cessation of his pain, and Claire, who is mainly inspired by belief in the better possibility). Because they are searching for directions to this alternative place, they are in the meantime wandering around lost; for that reason, their grasp of their situation is bound to be faulty. Traveling in this genre of film are thus characters whose particular traits and predicaments fit into this general framework of motives, pressures, and limitations. They are who the road is leading out.

As they follow this road, which takes them to places to which they are strangers, these protagonists meet other strangers, in unforeseeable ways. This sets up the central turn in the journey. It is always semi-comic and principally involves two people. (The works written with Shepard involve successions of dancing pairs: that is, Travis-Walt, Travis-Hunter, Travis-Jane; and Howard-his mother, Howard-Doreen, Howard-Earl, Howard-Sky.) The turn, like Epicurus's swerve, leads these people not only into each other, but also to become entangled. The comedy is not only that this happens by chance rather than by anyone's design, but also that at least one of the pair is positively uninterested in entering into any relationship at the time, let alone this particular one; he—it is always a he—just wants to be left alone. But despite these intentions, after the surprising appearance of the other and the circumstances that force the two for a time to be in each other's company, they cannot help but join in a call-and-response conversation that neither controls, but that grows and grows. It is as if each of their slightest actions, indeed their very bodies, emit signals to their partner that fuel a dialogue of misunderstanding and clarification, of constant surprise and negotiation. Before long, they have become part of something larger than each of them and more powerful than their wills.

In the middle of the journey, then, the protagonists approach an insight into themselves. They begin to realize that compared to this conversation in which they are participants, their separate, individual life is a small thing. Their general anxiety that this life is being wasted, and their particular concerns through which this restlessness expresses itself, no longer appear to them so pressing. Although they have not yet found that dream place and situation that would secure meaning for their singular lives, they start to let go of their worry about self-possession and self-importance. The fears they were fleeing turn out to be predicated on pretensions they can abandon. The latter is what their road leads them from.

But it does not follow that the protagonists can therefore live without a sense of purpose. The gist of the film's turn is, rather, that this purpose ends up being something that is impossible to find—it finds them. It does this precisely through the unintended conversation that draws them, even if unwillingly at first, on to a road they share. What then saves them from their wandering and brings it to a close turns out to be their communion that can inspire and sustain devotion over time. Their anxiety about the meaning of their mortal lives may in this way be displaced by their readiness to give those lives to, to die for, a community that is potentially immortal. Accordingly, it is to family, and the home its members take care of and so live meaningfully in, that this road leads the protagonists.

Now I hasten to underscore the obvious: family and home here are less concrete entities than figures of a kind of aspiration. We can easily think of quite different films in which the home is a prison pitting tormented and tormenting family members against each other until a lucky one breaks free. (The first one that pops into my mind is Robert Redford's *Ordinary People* (1980).) Some of these works drape their psychodramas in naturalistic detail and the rhetoric of realism. Their opposite is another kind of film whose tone is less shockingly matter-of-fact than wistful; I am thinking in particular of Ozu's oeuvre. It views the family home as a lost Eden. The Wenders road movie departs from both of these models. Unlike the first, it is not that interested in portraying how families really are as opposed to how they are supposed to be; it pretty much lacks any demystifying impulse. Instead, it tries forthrightly to imagine what building together a community might look like along the metaphorical lines of the family home. It is this orientation to the future that, secondly, distinguishes the Wenders road movie from Ozu's example. For Wenders, family is not rooted in childhood. Echoing the character Sky, who like others in the films did not grow up with all of her parents or siblings, it is not a matter of some gene determining the family's members but of some person deciding to say yes to a conversation into which he or she has fallen. This means that the members' bond is based less on a bygone past and more on how a history opens up possible directions for their ongoing lives. This promise that we spy in our relatedness and our cherishing of it is what gives the Wenders family a utopian, mythic quality. There are no limits to who can belong to it. And turning Hassan's line in *Land of Plenty* around a bit, I would add that wherever there is family, that place is home. There, relatives can publicly celebrate and cultivate its appearing.

Once the road has led the protagonists to this destination, how do they figure out concrete ways to devote themselves to it? How do they set aside their self-centeredness so that they can, over a lifetime of dedicated effort and specific actions, eventually die for their family home? Is it, for example, through some kind of broadly philosophical or other analysis of their situation? On the contrary, I have been contending that they achieve this through the composing and telling of their stories. Phillip, Travis, and Gene are engaged in doing this literally; Bruno, Robert, and Howard and his children appear to be involved in doing it more implicitly. Paul and Lana revise their stories in the light of their witnessing, and hearing from Youssef, Hassan's story. In effect, I understand Wenders to be offering a distinctive account of the catalyzing agent in these people's lives of awakening and conversion. It is not a singular, epiphanic moment of understanding in which, from some vantage point detached from the habits and interests that entrap one, one sees in a flash what one ought to do and how one ought to change, a moment that transforms one from Saul into Paul. Instead, what changes one's life is one's gradually developing capacity over time to tell, to oneself and to one's relatives, a story of the road one has been on and on which one met one's family. This story is about someone who was in flight from, yet still lost in, a life that lacked meaning. This person ran into another and both entered into a conversation that led them out. It drew them away from their attachment to their individual selves and, instead, toward their family home, whose approach they celebrate in story.

This destiny story that constitutes the road's destination, then, knits together the past, momentary experiences and actions of its protagonist into a whole. This unity is mortal in that it is shadowed by experiences not had and actions not done, never; it is a history of finitude. Continuing beyond the past, however, the story is also by necessity open-ended: nothing is at all certain about where it is going. It leads the protagonist only to the moment of its composing and telling, thus leaving him or her still in the middle of the journey. At the same time, it is this very open-endedness that broaches a direction for that person's entire life to follow through on. Instead of stepping back detachedly in order to deliberate about the truth, the protagonist takes the next step forward along the road he or she has already been true to. The destiny story thus makes it possible for one to distinguish adventure from directionless wandering: the former is a matter of one throwing oneself into the unknown future with the full force of a coherent life behind one, as if one were dancing a single continuous lifelong action. Furthermore, the story links that adventure, not to mention its protagonist, to relatives who, in effect, have called for it and to still others who will be called by its telling; one's dance, so to speak, takes place with partners. Hence because the adventure is not about self-centered derring-do, but about sacrificial care for a family, the protagonist's mortal life backward and forward is charged with meaning.

Such is the narrative form of the Wenders road movie. As he has elaborated it over the course of his career, its mythic elements have become clearer and its dramas more focused and powerfully concise. The films are no longer meandering; not only do they unfold their stories straightforwardly, but some of the later ones also employ chases to evoke deadlines and enhance suspense and liveliness. They stress that something is at stake in our experience of time. Now unfortunately, this has come at the expense of the earlier films' eye for stray happenings on the road; Wenders has made up for this somewhat by shifting this particular kind of attentiveness to his work in documentary. I have to say I rather mourn this change, though, because in transplanting the type of images of appearing we find in *Alice in the Cities* to a different register, their redemptive meaning becomes harder to appreciate. Meanwhile, in the road movies, the opposition to media images has been taken over almost entirely by the film's story; increasingly left aside is the search for counterimagery. I am not sure that this particular simplification of the form actually strengthens it. This criticism aside, I am nevertheless convinced that the destiny story he developed is insightfully groundbreaking. We see this when we compare it to related narrative genres.

* * *

The road movie genre as a whole emerged in the United States in the late sixties. Furnishing the conditions for it were the development of an extensive, cross-country highway system; the presence of large areas of unspoiled land; the general availability and popularity of automobiles in this prosperous era; and, last but not least, cheap gas. All of these things meant that the pleasures of driving long distances were already familiar to many Americans and were simply waiting for their definitive cultural expression. The mother that ultimately gave birth to the road movie, however, was that period's youth counterculture. From the start, the genre was marked by that culture's concerns and dreams and its historical development followed that culture's fortunes. Starting on a note of exuberant release, like a good piece of rock and roll, it had become by the end of the seventies a vehicle for conveying a pervasive malaise of drifting disillusionment. In the eighties, road movies began to mock self-reflexively their own countercultural stereotypes in the playfully ironic, sometimes cynical manner of postmodernism. Since the nineties, some of that self-consciousness has abated as the genre has expanded to include stories rooted in other communities and places besides white America.[1]

If we focus on works of its classical period, we may observe, following David Laderman, that there are two main strands to the genre. The first consists of sometimes horrifyingly violent stories about outlaws: familiar examples include *Bonnie and Clyde*, *Badlands*, and *The Sugarland Express* (1973). The second strand is centered more on various kinds of adventurers, albeit often quite anti-heroic ones: we might think of those in *The Rain People* (1969), *Five Easy Pieces* (1970), and *Two-Lane Blacktop* (1971). To be sure, Laderman acknowledges that this division is a slight, heuristic exaggeration; most of the genre's protagonists are to different degrees both outlaws and adventurers and their stories combine features from each strand.[2] This is above all the case in Dennis Hopper's 1969 film, *Easy Rider*, surely the road movie's Colossus.

The film recounts how Wyatt, aka Captain America, and a latter-day Billy the Kid journey together from Mexico and then Los Angeles across the country to New Orleans. Each is driving a dazzling motorcycle stuffed with cash made from a drug deal, in the film's prologue. They are on their way to join the city's famous Mardi Gras festival. Along this road, they give lifts first to one guy and then to another who accompany them for parts of the trip. Their travel takes them to episodic stops at an Indian campsite, a hippie commune, a small-town jail, and a brothel, among other places; most of it passes through wide-open, breathtakingly scenic vistas, including, of course, Ford's Monument Valley. Like the Western hero, they make their home the indefinite frontier between civilization and nature. The road comes to an abrupt end, however, when they encounter on a lonely stretch a couple of rednecks in a pickup who reply to an insult by Billy by gunning both of them down.

Obviously, this is the barest of bare-bone summaries of a film that I am counting on to be familiar to many. My hope is simply that these plot points may serve as an *aide memoire* for evoking the work's outlaw and adventurer elements. Wyatt and Billy are outlaws not only literally in their criminal scheme, but also more generally in the way their whole lifestyle expresses the spirit of rebellion. Their long hair and dress, their insouciance and irreverence, their

---

[1] This capsule history of the road movie is indebted to Neil Archer, *The Road Movie: In Search of Meaning* (New York: Columbia University Press, 2016); and David Laderman, *Driving Visions: Exploring the Road Movie* (Austin: University of Texas Press, 2002).
[2] See Laderman, *Driving Visions*, 20.

self-sufficient and nomadic way of life: all of this proclaims their freedom from convention and routine. They are actively and publicly rejecting the normal trappings of an American man of the time. And why do they do this? I think for two reasons. On the one hand, they have become outlaws because they have been cast out: they are responding to their ostracism by their frightened, resentful, and contemptuously bigoted fellow citizens. Their rebellion is partly suffered. But on the other hand, they are also inspired by a more positive spirit of exploration. They see in the unknown country the possibility of a utopian alternative. They experience direct intimations of this in the excitements of speed and psychedelic sensuality and in the magical workings of chance. Their trip, far from being simply a means to get to a set place, is the very process of the self discovering the authentic ends of its life. And of it joining the counter-community that shares a commitment to this discovery.

But as I have noted, the journey terminates in violent death. Wyatt and Billy's rebellion is not capable of overcoming the superior force of establishment society. Moreover, their adventurousness is likewise all too weak. Despite the work they have poured into stylizing their lives, their drug-running is at bottom a business like any other, one that conserves the rules and hierarchies of capitalism. And what their drug taking and other explorations of pleasure expand, more than consciousness, is the passivity and market of consumerism. No wonder, then, that Wyatt's famous last line is, "We blew it." Rather than feeling that their murder comes entirely out of the blue, we are apt to experience it as a shocking, but nevertheless fitting punctuation for a tragedy. Their story of travel, rebellion, and adventure going nowhere is bound to end with fate.

Evidently, the Wenders road movie is a child of *Easy Rider*. It is marked by features of both the traveling outlaw and the adventurer. But the outlaw side of the equation has diminished to a minimum. Although Wenders's protagonists are, indeed, fleeing from the conventional ways of life offered them, they take much less rebellious pride in this rejection. They run away from normal society without expressly challenging it to change, let alone slaughtering its members as in some other outlaw films. Conversely, that society is not threatened by them nor does it feel any urgency to rein them in. In general, the Wenders protagonist starts off on a much less secure footing than cocky Wyatt and Billy; he or she is more introspectively worried about his or her own inner strength.

Along these lines, while this protagonist is definitely on the adventurer side of the spectrum, his or her quest has an edge of desperation that takes it beyond simple exploration. Because Wenders's characters are more preoccupied with being lost, they are rather less open to the passing delights of strong sensation and the alternative modes of being alive to the world they can intimate. I am talking about matters of degree here, but as an illustration, a marvelous moment in *Land of Plenty* comes to mind. On her drive with Paul to Trona, Lana at one point sticks her arm out of the window and lets it gently caress the breeze up and down (Figure 3.1). This gesture recalls some of the more flamboyant hijinks of the characters in the American film, all the little dances they do on their bikes as they speed into the wind. What is striking, though, is how exceptional this kind of fun is in Wenders's work. (The motorcycle ride in *Kings of the Road* also echoes *Easy Rider*, of course, but in a more muted way.) Nor are his protagonists likely to be carried away by grand visions of a radically different world, and this is not merely because getting stoned is not their thing. Once again, the kind of extroverted self-confidence that Wyatt and Billy radiate is precisely what these protagonists most feelingly lack.

As I noted, however, there is one road movie by Wenders that is anomalous in this regard. *Lisbon Story*, released in 1994, picks up the saga of Phillip Winter from when it left off at the end of *Alice*. Phillip is now a movie soundman. Returning home after a protracted visit elsewhere, with a leg in a cast, he discovers that a filmmaker friend of his, Friedrich, has sent him a postcard

Figure 3.1 *Land of Plenty* directed by Wim Wenders © Reverse Angle/IFC Films/InDigEnt 2004. All rights reserved.

urgently calling for help.³ Unhesitatingly, Phillip sets off from Frankfurt with a car full of equipment to aid his pal in Lisbon. It quickly becomes clear that this Phillip is no longer the lost soul of the earlier film, but someone more comfortably happy-go-lucky as he speeds across a newly borderless Europe.

What ensues is a light, droll adventure. On the road to Portugal, Phillip's automobile, in stages, falls apart. It is only because he is able to trade one of the last things in the car that still works, the radio, for a lift from a truck driver, that he finally makes it to the house in which Friedrich is staying. The latter, though, has mysteriously disappeared. Phillip's journey turns into a quest to find the man who had brought him there. After settling into Friedrich's place, he discovers silent footage of the movie the latter has been shooting, and so as he wanders around the city looking for the man, limping on his cast, he also records sounds for the film. He is sometimes joined in his walks and work by a group of kids whom Friedrich has befriended, and he regularly encounters an enigmatic boy he suspects is connected to Friedrich, who flees him. He begins reading the books of Pessoa left on the bed table. For three weeks, Phillip swims around thus in the wake of his friend's life and world. The episodes of his time in Lisbon are marked by a steady stream of gags and humorous digressions, as well as punctual moments of naturally happening beauty that are the equal of those in *Alice*. At no point, though, does the now older man appear troubled about the direction of his life. Furthermore, he is remarkably open to, and interested in, the people he meets.

Eventually, Phillip runs into Friedrich. The latter has abandoned his film and filmmaking; he despairs of its images that he sees now function to sell things. Recall that the younger Phillip in *Alice* was preoccupied with the same insight. Friedrich's reaction to it is to embark on a project of blindly, without looking or any guiding intention at all, videotaping the city as he walks, John Cage-style. In this fashion, he hopes to produce and amass images that, because they remain unseen even by their recorder, are purified of any commercial impulse. Phillip responds to this as his trip's ultimate joke. Effortlessly and without encountering any resistance, he gets his lost friend to trust his eyes again, despite their fall from innocence, and believe in the traditional beauty

---

³ This character has the same name as the film director protagonist in Wenders's *The State of Things* (1982) and is played by the same actor. In some ways, his predicament echoes that of his namesake. Indeed, *Lisbon Story* can be seen as a redemptive rewriting of the earlier film's bleak ending.

of moving pictures. The last we see of the two characters, they are back on the street, antically trying to catch on film the life of Lisbon.

As I hope this brief reading indicates, what separates this film from Wenders's other road movies is that there is no question of Phillip affirming his destiny. He travels to Lisbon and moves around the city, but he is not led out anywhere. For the most part, he is unchanged by his visit. He is concerned about Friedrich, but because nothing shows that his friend is in immediate danger, he does not feel that anything crucial is at stake in his day-to-day experiences. In his journey, he encounters surprising breakdowns, absences, and irritations, but of a comic, mosquito-like scale. In contrast, oddly enough, the man he is searching for is undergoing a more dramatic crisis. At stake in Friedrich's doubts about filmmaking does appear to be something like his destiny. However, *Lisbon Story* portrays this crisis with so little pathos, and resolves it so easily, that it, in effect, reduces it to yet another funny turn.

One thing, though, adds a touch of somberness to this otherwise cheerful adventure. In a key scene, Phillip is at work on Friedrich's film when he hears some music emanating from another part of the house. Drawn to it, he discovers the building's owners, the band Madredeus, rehearsing in a room. They welcome him and invite him to stay for another song. As he listens to "Ainda," a crystalline piece of *fado*, Phillip gazes faraway into himself, deeply touched. He conceives a passion for the music, which sometimes accompanies his views of the city, and for the lead singer, Teresa, who is always leaving. The hopelessness of the latter and the power of the former to recall him to life's finitude infuse his growing love of Lisbon (Figure 3.2). Even as *Lisbon Story* departs from Wenders's other road movies, then, it cannot help but at least allude to, longingly, the unpursued theme of destiny.

So much for this unusual entry in Wenders's oeuvre. Let me return in summary to the comparison of the classic road movie, *Easy Rider*, to Wenders's more typical ones. Departing from the disparity between the self-confident protagonists of the former and the more doubting ones of the latter, their narrative arcs move in close to opposite directions. As I summarized, the former film is a tragedy: the contradictions implicit in Wyatt and Billy's rebellion and exploration gradually work their way to the surface and summon their fate on the road. Their story is that of a fall from grace. In contrast, Wenders's films summon a surprising destiny to the rescue of their already fallen protagonists; their endings are not disastrous but redemptive. When I

Figure 3.2 *Lisbon Story* directed by Wim Wenders © Road Movies Filmproduktion, Berlin 1994. All rights reserved.

turn shortly to compare these works to film noir, I shall discuss in more detail the opposition between fate and destiny. For now, let me simply register the difference between most mainstream road movies that chart the sobering yet, for all that, quasi-heroic defeat of their flawed but courageous nonconformists, and the Wenders road movie that saves, if only provisionally, its protagonist through the appearing of family and home. As I shall also elaborate later, this suggests that this protagonist, unlike his or her more mainstream relatives, is more precisely neither an outlaw nor an adventurer. He or she is someone being educated.

* * *

Suppose, then, that the Wenders road movie is a vehicle for exploring the question and meaning of destiny in our lives. Why did it develop in the direction of narrative fiction? Why did Wenders not, instead, work with accounts of actual travel? Granted that his films were shaped by all sorts of historical contingencies in addition to the idiosyncrasies of his taste; nevertheless, does it make retrospective sense that fiction may have appeared to him richer in vivid possibilities for exploring this subject than any other rhetorical language?

To pursue this question for the purpose of unearthing more of the distinctive nature and power of the destiny story, let me take a quick look at the travelogue film genre. A work of this kind is usually made for television;

I think in particular of Michael Palin's various series of this genre for the BBC, which have enjoyed popular success. At its center is a factual road journey. How does the film capture our attention and absorb us in this trip? It achieves this principally by weaving together in a mutually reinforcing fashion our interest in four elements. First, there are the visually exotic, sometimes stunningly beautiful locales visited that represent escapes from our familiar world. The camera alternately contemplates, probes, and caresses these vistas, encouraging us to marvel at their features. At the same time, secondly, we are usually supplied with a fair amount of information about them to listen to; much of this is historical in nature. It explains why a particular locale is not only beautiful but also important and famous; to make this knowledge less dry and more accessible, it is often associated with the exploits of characters with whom we can to some degree identify. Indeed, since the overarching theme of my book is education, it is worth underscoring that the travelogue is in this manner appealing to the viewer's interest in learning. From this follows a third focus of interest: whenever there is learning going on, there is normally at its center a teacher. In this kind of film, this position is occupied by the narrator, an explorer, interviewer, and raconteur who is especially charming. He or she combines enthusiastic curiosity and impressive perceptiveness with winning friendliness. Finally, this pedagogical work takes us to the fourth focal point: the events of the journey to and from these locales. Although it is not always the case, some of these journeys involve the narrator, not to mention his or her crew, in some adversity; how this is conquered becomes part of what makes the film interesting. All in all, the travelogue enables its viewers to go on a diverting sightseeing voyage from the comfort of their living rooms.

If we accept this as a rough outline of the genre, we could imagine a work in it that added one more feature. Supplementing the film's four points of interest would be some musings on the narrator's part about destiny. Rather than merely tossing in a few ornamental words on this topic, let us imagine that he or she makes it clear that either the destiny of the narrator or that of a central historical character is what the entire film is about. In this fashion, the work could directly and explicitly explain to its viewers what is only suggested in the Wenders road movie. Why, then, do we not see more travelogue films of this kind in existence? Or even, to my knowledge, a single one?

My conjecture is that the topic of destiny is, in fact, not so easily combinable with the travelogue's other elements. This is suggested to me when I consider one of Wenders's non-road-movie works, *Tokyo-ga*, which came out in 1985. Now I am quite aware that it is a bit unfair to call this documentary a travelogue. As we would expect from a work by the director of *Alice in the Cities*, it is self-consciously hostile to anything that smacks of sightseeing. Even as it transports its viewers to Tokyo, it engages them in critical reflection on contradictory images of the city and its inhabitants, speaking moreover in a searching, personal voice. We are never encouraged simply to escape into the delights of the famous and remote other. Despite all that, though, Wenders employs most of the genre's distinctive and elemental rhetorical conventions; for this reason, perhaps we could call his work an anti-travelogue. This quality makes it an especially good test case: it adopts the travelogue form for a purpose more serious than that of tourism. Knowing what we do about his interest in destiny, then, I want to examine briefly how his use of this form's conventions, like any tool, appears to extract practical concessions that hinder his capacity to pursue this interest in this particular work. The film sheds speculative light, at least, on the gap that separates the travelogue from the destiny story and on why the latter might lend itself more naturally to fiction.

Tokyo-ga opens with an evocation, in the most stirring terms, of the "sacred treasure of cinema" bequeathed to us by the director Yasujiro Ozu. It inspired Wenders, he declares in the film's voiceover, to travel to Tokyo to see if the place currently resembles in any way its images in the master's films. He is searching for confirmation that Ozu captured an enduring truth. Soon after Wenders arrives, though, he finds himself swimming in media images pouring out of the city's pores. Ozu's pictures of families navigating tensions reproduced from generation to generation, tensions distinctively sharpened by the modernization and Americanization of the streets in which they walk, now appears to have been utterly displaced by a bewildering labyrinth of simulacra. This postmodern metropolis resists coherent depiction because it is largely made up of simulated experiences that, while compensating for the absence of the real thing, hypnotically distract and fragment us (Figure 3.3). The more closely Wenders pays attention, however, the more he slips into Ozu's peaceful acceptance that even as parts of traditional Japan continue to pass away, this time because of postmodernization, underneath is still the same old parade of generations living in the embrace of cherry blossoms and raven calls (Figure 3.4). The story of Wenders's trip is thus one about finding in Tokyo, after all, traces of Ozu's families, both the ones that were in front of

Genre Contrasts 87

Figure 3.3 *Tokyo-ga* directed by Wim Wenders © Road Movies Filmproduktion, Berlin/Chris Sievernich Produktion, Berlin/Gray City Inc. 1985. All rights reserved.

Figure 3.4 *Tokyo-ga* directed by Wim Wenders © Road Movies Filmproduktion, Berlin/Chris Sievernich Produktion, Berlin/Gray City Inc. 1985. All rights reserved.

the camera and the one behind that made the films. Not unlike in Wenders's road movies, home is still recognizable, even when it houses masses absorbed by their screens.

In the course of this journey, Wenders cannot help but stress images of exotic Japan. We are shown pachinko parlors, video game arcades, surreal golf ranges without golf holes, uncanny wax food, teenagers aping American greasers, and, naturally, ludicrous television ads. All of this pushes the point, common in all travelogues, that we should be amazed at Tokyo, even if also a little alarmed by it. Accompanying this imagery, as we would also expect, is verbal information about Ozu's world, concerns, and work, which affirms the historical significance of what we are looking at. And as the teacher, Wenders is perfect: eloquent, ruminative, good-humored, and engaging. What a stark contrast he makes to the standoffish, if impressive, Werner Herzog, hectoring us atop the Tokyo Tower. Finally, although Wenders's journey does not require him to rise to any physical challenges, we do watch and listen to him struggle with his allergy to the postmodern image world. His overcoming of this resistance—in contrast, Herzog, in the scene above, flat-out condemns that world—through an emulation of Ozu's example, especially the way the latter cultivates infectiously a kind of counterdramatic, unshakeable and calming affection for his characters and the life that surrounds them, makes for a compelling story.

But it is not quite about destiny. In particular, the story does not tell us about how either the images of postmodern Tokyo or the Tokyo of Ozu's films make a real difference to Wenders's life, let alone to ours. He declares that he is appalled by the first and reveres the second, and he offers us some explanation of why, but we do not see how these inclinations lead him to live his life in a particular way. And how could we? The focus of the travelogue film, even in this self-critical variant, has to be on what objectively exists independent of any subjective views about it; this is what it means for the work to assert its nonfictional, primarily documentary nature. It is, above all, about a place or places. In contrast, the road movie puts that nature and place in the service of an exercise of imagination. Yes, there is still attention to the external world of things, but that world is at bottom a stage for dramatizing plausibly a character's internal struggles to live a worthwhile life. As we viewers try to piece together and understand the events and actions depicted in the film as such a drama, unconstrained by any interest in whether it happened in fact, we are invited to draw, and reflect, on our own stories and how they compare. We become more attuned to the idea that what matters about a place to which we have journeyed is not, as in a travelogue, its exotic beauty and historical importance, factors which are often of interest to us precisely because they carry us away from our routines, but, rather, in how it plays a part in the inner realization of our destiny. Our passion for this meaning is so much stronger than curiosity or the need for a dose of stimulation. Accordingly, it is only after I have sympathized with what it means to Claire to become hooked on her dream images, or to Phillip to take up his camera again and snap a family-looking group on the ferry boat, sympathized because I can recognize my own struggles in their stories, that I can truly understand what Ozu means for Wenders. And prior to such sympathy, it is unlikely that adding reflections on Ozu, or even on how Ozu can be someone's destiny, to a travelogue film will bring home this idea to me or any other viewer in as moving a way. For this reason, then, I find it hard to avoid the thought that Wenders's road was bound to lead to the road movie.

* * *

What is the difference between destiny and fate? In what sense is the Wenders road movie anti-fatalistic? To explore these questions and the way they oppose Wenders's mini-genre to film noir, I turn to two works. One of them starts off as something of a proto-road movie and turns into a noir. The other is a noir by Wenders that unsurprisingly bears some of the features of his road movies. As conventions of both genres enter into proximity to each other in these films, the genres' contrasting attitudes toward death become visible.

Let me take as my point of departure some of the usual things we associate with the concept of fate. This concept is naturally rooted in the fatal, that is, death. Death is understood to be the ultimate loss of everything, the ultimate catastrophe. It can be avoided only temporarily; for a mortal to live in time, accordingly, is for that person to be concerned with deferring death. To prolong our lives, we each struggle to gain control over them and the world. This overarching endeavor, not to mention the specific projects that contribute to it, requires that we assume we are centers of effective and rationally improvable action. Now fate is a name for that force that subverts this assumption. Specifically, it subjects us to a kind of cosmic irony that twists our actions so that they eventually result in the opposite of what we ultimately intended. What we do to prolong our lives and distance ourselves from death ends up being the very vehicle that effectively delivers us to it. When we realize this tragedy, we recognize that our attempts to master our lives were mere hubris; all along, we were slaves to fate that leads us in the course of time to doom.

As many have observed, film noir constitutes one such tragic form of experience; Robert Pippin's discussion of this in *Fatalism in American Film*

Noir is especially perceptive and I draw on it in my summary here.[4] This genre is composed of a framework of conventions that enhances the expressive power of a story about fate. One element of this framework is a social world that is the antithesis of meliatory and just. Viewed through a lens of disillusionment, it is, rather, one that is fixed and corrupt; indeed, under the surface and at its core is criminal violence. Furthermore, inhabiting this world are people whose identities are shadowy. The only thing we know for sure about them, the films tell us again and again, is that they are not who they seem to be. And in the thick of the main group of characters, of course, is the femme fatale: she who promises happiness, but who really brings corruption and catastrophe. In the course of many of the classic noirs, she leads the central protagonist to a moment when he composes and tells a story about his fate.

In this last respect, film noir intriguingly echoes the Wenders road movie in that both often culminate in stories that the protagonists relate. What, then, are some of the characteristics of the fate story that distinguish it from the destiny one? In narrating his fate, the noir protagonist looks back on his life retrospectively from the vantage point of its imminent end. He reviews what has already taken place and cannot be changed; these events form an inevitable road to death. At the same time, his story rhetorically emphasizes the blindness and impotence of his various actions along this road as he tried to improvise responses to the things that befell him. And once more, the main thing that befell him was the femme fatale; his story accordingly also affirms her superior, manipulative power. In effect, the story argues that not only can things no longer be changed at the moment of its telling, but also they never really could have been changed even during the time of their happening. No matter how much he tried to do the right and rational thing, it was simply impossible for the protagonist's actions to make a difference and overcome a superior, external power. In spite of this, though, at the center of the story he composes to stress all this, there is the stark fact that he did do at least one thing that matters: he killed someone (and perhaps multiple others). The fate story thus functions as both a confession of guilt and a plea for exculpation: this murder that he committed, he did not *really* do—fate did. The story expresses the protagonist's own ambiguous, possibly self-delusive identity.

---

[4] See Robert B. Pippin, *Fatalism in American Film Noir: Some Cinematic Philosophy* (Charlottesville: University of Virginia Press, 2012).

We see all these conventions at work in Edgar G. Ulmer's 1945 film, *Detour*. It opens with footage of a road unrolling behind a car's back windshield. We are watching what a traveler is leaving behind and fleeing from. At the risk of anachronism, I am tempted to say so far, so Wenders-road-movie-like. What brings on the distinctive noir rain, so to speak, is the next episode, which takes place at a roadside diner. The touchy, unstable protagonist, Al, suddenly causes a scene when he vehemently objects to a love song that one of the customers has put on the jukebox. Al hears that song as one of doom. His shadowy ambiguity revealed, he proceeds to tell a typically confessional and exculpatory flashback fate story about his trip.

What is this story about? Since it most obviously concerns a journey from New York to Los Angeles, I can summarize it using the quartet of questions I have been addressing to Wenders's road movies. Who is being led out on this trip? It is Al, a piano player who is trying to get to happiness with his girlfriend, Sue. She is a singer who separated from him in order to pursue a career boost in Hollywood, but whom he now is determined to marry. From where is he being led? Even as his hitchhiking is taking him closer to his goal, it is actually drawing him away from his love. By this cruel irony, we recognize the road as one of fate. To where is he being led instead? He is being drawn to apparent murder, entanglement with another woman, and the fear and resignation that follow in their wake. After being picked up by a driver named Charles, he does something that may have caused Charles's death, it is not clear. In his narration of the scene, Al admits that it looks like he killed Charles but claims that it was really an accident; because of the unreliability built into these stories, we are not sure whether we are watching what happened or what Al is saying happened. In addition, it is also possible that Charles was already dead prior to Al's actions. Al, furthermore, rationalizes why he then goes on to assume Charles's identity and take possession of his car and money. In this guise, resuming his journey, he picks up a hitchhiker, Vera. She recognizes that he is not who he pretends to be, however, because earlier in her journey she had fended off the real Charles's advances. By threatening to tell the authorities that Al murdered Charles, she gains leverage over him. Soon, they are living together in an LA apartment while she plots for them to swindle money from Charles's father. In the course of desperately trying to get away from her or persuade her not to insist on this criminal scheme, Al accidentally kills her, too. So, at least, we are again told. His story ends as he awaits his inevitable capture by the police, who, he is certain, will refuse to believe him and sentence him to death. What, then, is finally leading him to this finale? I suspect it is a guilt that the road summons up and that Vera personifies. Perhaps Al knows in his heart that he does not really love Sue. When Charles dies in his company, he jumps at the chance to follow his desire to be someone else. And when Vera appears on the road, he lets this Charles persona, which has become rather dissociated from him, be attracted to her, just as Charles was earlier. Indeed, even as she uses his presumed guilt for Charles's murder as leverage to keep him under her thumb, he uses her entrapment of him as a baffle that enables him to be unaware of his attraction. In which case, it would seem, the towering femme fatale comes down demystified to Al's wayward desire. He tells a fate story ultimately, if obliquely, to the Sue in his mind so that he can exorcize his apparent guilt and repress his real one.

At any event, what makes this film not a Wenders road movie but a noir, I find, is its attitude toward death. In a fate story, death is something that I as the protagonist must suffer. It comes to me as punishment for a murder I half committed, half was roped into and went along with. The road of my fate, then, is a chain of twists and capitulations on my part that leads me to my end. In contrast, in a destiny story, my dying can be a lifelong activity of giving my life for something. It is inspired by love not of a spider woman, but of a family home. The road of destiny is thus a chain of twists and affirmations leading to an ongoing invention of the way forward. Indeed, more than its comparative optimism, what opposes destiny to fate is that the former has no place for a story of the true, overwhelming determinism of death. Destiny, instead, celebrates the fictionalization of life more completely and consistently. *Detour* turns away from this road.

So too does the road in Wenders's 1977 noir, *The American Friend*. On it are two protagonists who in certain respects resemble those in Wenders's road movies. How these characteristics in them end up being twisted in typical film noir directions sheds additional light on the clash between the genres. In particular, this film suggests that the dissociative gap between a noir protagonist's fatalism and the actions for which he is responsible means that a fate story can be about someone, even about oneself, but it cannot be a story one wholeheartedly authors. It cannot be one's story.

The first protagonist is Jonathan, an ordinary picture framer and family man in Hamburg who is suffering from an illness that he fears will soon take his life. After he refuses to shake the hand of a visiting art dealer, Tom, the latter passes Jonathan's name on to a gangster associate, Minot. Minot fabricates a telegram and some medical examination results to make it seem to Jonathan that his illness is, indeed, in its terminal stage. He then offers to pay Jonathan a pile of money if Jonathan kills a gangster, or possibly two. Minot sells this deal by asking Jonathan if he would not want to provide for his family after he is gone. In effect, he is appealing to Jonathan's desire to make a positive difference to those he loves who will live on. He evidently recognizes that Jonathan is worried that his life will pass away meaninglessly; indeed, in one vignette, Jonathan lies awake at night wondering if his son will even remember him. In this film, then, the same existential anxiety and quest for meaning that sends Wenders's road movie protagonists on their journeys sends Jonathan on his.

Jonathan accepts Minot's deal for the sake of his family—this ironically exiles him from home. Why is this? I think it is because Jonathan's desire to die meaningfully for those he loves is quickly perverted and eclipsed by a related one that is much more ignoble. We see this when, after sleepwalking and stumbling through his first murder, he lights up at the realization that he is going to get away with it (Figure 3.5). I suspect that his exultation is due to more than just relief that he has preserved his own life. He realizes that rather than simply submitting to death, let alone accepting it as a condition for his life taking a sacrificial form, he can actually master it, at least momentarily, by

Figure 3.5 *The American Friend* directed by Wim Wenders © Road Movies Filmproduktion, Berlin/Wim Wenders Produktion, Munich/Les Films du Losange, Paris/Westdeutscher Rundfunk, Cologne 1977. All rights reserved.

dishing it out to someone else. He can be death. Although he never ceases in the film to be sickened by this power, he also becomes addicted to it.

As Jonathan plunges deeper into darkness, he is almost rescued by the film's other protagonist, Tom. At first, Tom is nothing but a narcissist empty of moral scruples. He is utterly rootless, lost, and wandering. (Played by Dennis Hopper, he at one point steps out on to his porch and begins singing to the world "Ballad of Easy Rider.") After he takes revenge for Jonathan's slight to his vanity by setting up Jonathan with Minot, however, Tom falls for his part into a surprising infatuation with Jonathan. The stable and responsible father and craftsman seems to possess the secret to happiness. When Tom learns from Minot that Jonathan is about to go through with a second murder on a train, he unexpectedly shows up at Jonathan's side to help him. After they have repulsed an attack by additional gangsters, he takes charge and comes up with a plan to dispose of all the bodies. They will together drive them some distance from Hamburg to a deserted beach by the North Sea. His attachment to Jonathan and his joy at working with him is written all over his face (Figure 3.6). Thus over the course of the film, his self-centeredness begins to yield, in true Wendersian fashion, to a commitment to a shared road and purpose.

In the end, though, Jonathan double-crosses his American friend *fatal* and this seals his, and Tom's, fate. He deserts Tom on the beach with the corpses, escaping from them with his wife, and drives for home. Before he reaches it, however, he has a terminal stroke on the road. Although it is not clear whether

Figure 3.6 *The American Friend* directed by Wim Wenders © Road Movies Filmproduktion, Berlin/Wim Wenders Produktion, Munich/Les Films du Losange, Paris/Westdeutscher Rundfunk, Cologne 1977. All rights reserved.

it was his illness or something else that causes his death, the event confirms the tragic form of this noir. The very action that Jonathan at last takes to break free of his doom leads him finally to it. And the same goes for Tom. The very action he takes to forge a friendship with Jonathan drives him away. Dispossessed of their actions as these turn into the wheels and cogs of fate, these protagonists' ability to compose a destiny story is hence deactivated; this may be why they do not tell any story in this film. Indeed, because they were both responding chiefly to a need for meaning rather than one to deny their guilt, it is hard to imagine what they could possibly find satisfying about a fate story. Instead, in the very last shot of him perched alone on a lifeguard tower, Tom simply sings a bit of Bob Dylan's "I Pity the Poor Immigrant," a lament for a meaningless life.

What finally distinguishes a destiny story from a fate story is the activity of responsible authorship that gives birth to the former and that the former establishes. Such a story has the power to change its storyteller and thus be an education. For this to happen, though, the person has to appreciate what in it has come to him. Otherwise, the tale becomes one of an education manqué.

* * *

In 1975, Wenders released *Wrong Move* (Falsche Bewegung). This film is widely considered part of his "road trilogy," sandwiched between *Alice in the Cities* and *Kings of the Road*. Like the other two, it follows its protagonist on a journey, in this case down the length of Germany, and its story is composed of a series of leisurely paced episodes. I earlier noted that its screenplay, which was written by Handke, is based on Goethe's novel *Wilhelm Meister's Apprenticeship*.[5] The adaptation is quite loose, though, and the film's departures from the *Bildungsroman* disclose some additional distinctive traits of the Wenders road movie. Indeed, in a key respect, the divergence between the two works is so striking, we may more accurately describe *Wrong Move* as an anti-road-movie. In line with the project of this chapter, it exemplifies in a telling way what the Wenders road movie is not.

Following Goethe, Wenders names the main character Wilhelm. He is a young, would-be writer who is living with his mother in Glückstadt, which can be translated as "Happiness City." As someone decidedly unhappy, however, he is

---

[5] See Johann Wolfgang von Goethe, *Wilhelm Meister's Apprenticeship*, ed. and trans. Eric A. Blackall and Victor Lange (Princeton: Princeton University Press, 1989).

first introduced to us as he gazes out of his window, alone in his room, listening to The Troggs' "I Just Sing." He methodically repeats the record, cranks up the music, and suddenly punches out the glass, hurting himself. Although a neat and well-behaved man, he is dying to leave the town that gave him his manners and find his authentic self in the wild world beyond. He longs to be tested by unpredictable adventure so that he may cultivate the writing voice it draws out of him. In the meantime, he has withdrawn from others into silence, pouring his words and thoughts, instead, into a notebook. Quickly sketched thus at the film's start, Wilhem is a slightly silly, self-dramatizing romantic, resembling Phillip in *Alice*. Even as we may sympathize with his desire to live a life that is true to his individual experience, we are invited to smile at how Bovaryishly commonplace this desire is, a product of paperback books and sheltered fantasies.

With his mother's encouragement, though—and a train ticket she gives him to the place that happens to be the setting of the novel he is currently reading—Wilhelm embarks on a trip to Bonn. In typical Wenders road movie fashion, he encounters on his journey various people with whom he enters into conversation and who become attached to him. First, there is an older street musician, Laertes, and his companion, a mute girl who performs magic and gymnastic tricks, named Mignon. They push themselves on Wilhelm, appealing to him in so many words for shelter and support, and he does not resist. Then, there is an actress, Therese, who exchanges with him longing looks from a window on a train that runs alongside his for a while; after their tracks separate, she manages to get to him a message with her telephone number. At Bonn, they catch up with each other and she joins the group of him, Laertes, and Mignon. While the four of them are walking through the city, their number is supplemented by a young man from Austria, Bernhard. Like Wilhelm, he wants to write; inasmuch as his poems are so ludicrously clichéd, however, and his temper so good-naturedly gregarious, he represents something like Wilhelm's embarrassing mirror image. All of these people are rather abruptly and inexplicably attracted to Wilhelm: Laertes regards him as a kind of son; Mignon and Therese yearn and compete for his love; Bernhard looks for his approval as a fellow craftsman. Wilhelm passively accepts their company as if he is in a dream, and in Therese's car, they together decide on a whim to visit Bernhard's uncle. The formation of this seemingly hypnotized group around comic Wilhelm recalls in its surreal preposterousness the films of Luis Buñuel—a new departure for Wenders.

When they arrive at a decrepit, open villa, they are greeted by a man who Bernhard realizes is, in fact, not his uncle. They have driven to the wrong place. This person, who in the script is simply referred to as the Industrialist, is carrying a rifle; he explains that he was just about to shoot himself when he heard the automobile approaching, saving him. He invites everyone to be his house guests. Later that night, as they all sip wine in the living room, he holds forth on the problem of loneliness in Germany; he portrays the sentiment as a sort of self-conscious, theatrical acting-out of the self. (Listening to his rant, it is hard not to think of Handke's compatriot writer, Thomas Bernhard.) Eventually, everyone retires to various rooms upstairs. Wilhelm, searching in the dark for Therese, stumbles into a room occupied by Mignon and ends up sleeping with her. This is only his most obvious wrong move.

The next day, Wilhelm talks with members of the troupe in turn as they promenade along some hills overlooking the Rhine. Largely oblivious to the splendor of this expansive landscape with its autumnal colors, Wilhelm concentrates on fatherly Laertes's Nazi past and conceives of the wish to kill him. On the other hand, Therese puts Wilhelm on the defensive when she accuses him of coldly putting her off. And he is tickled by a haiku about love from Bernhard, but persists in not taking him seriously. These conversations, each inconclusive, begin to place Wilhelm in relationships with these people. Something in the would-be artist, however, keeps stubbornly disconnecting him from them and the world (Figure 3.7).

Figure 3.7 *Wrong Move* directed by Wim Wenders © Solaris Film, Munich/Westdeutscher Rundfunk, Cologne 1975. All rights reserved.

When the group returns to the villa, the characters all discover that the Industrialist, who boasted of being "proud with loneliness," has hung himself. In a demoralized panic, they get back on the road. At a rest stop, Bernhard, their disarming fool, abandons them. The remaining four drive to Therese's apartment on the outskirts of Frankfurt. In this sterile, suburban environment, Wilhelm again simmers with discontent; he bickers with Therese and makes a half-hearted attempt to throw the nonswimmer Laertes into a river, who then flees. Soon, Wilhelm decides to flee himself and breaks away from Therese and Mignon to take a trip to Germany's highest mountain, the Zugspitze. At the summit, he realizes that all this time he has been using his writing as a pretext to close himself off from the others. In particular, he threatened the old man instead of trying to understand him. He, too, has been killing himself out of pride. The film ends with him having a possibly breakthrough, possibly ironic, epiphany: "It came to me that I had missed out on something and was still missing out with every new move."

Wrong Move echoes *Wilhelm Meister's Apprenticeship* in numerous ways, but I want to focus on three fairly plain, principal ones. First of all, the two Wilhelms are pretty close to each other, if not quite identical. Both are youths who are drawn to artistic callings and adventurous travel. More than acquiring money and power, both are interested in developing their self-understanding, wisdom, and maturity, in *Bildung*. Goethe's protagonist, though, is rather more eager and naïve about what the next bend in the road will give him than Wenders's more desperate and timid Wilhelm. Secondly, the film's supporting characters are loose yet recognizable composites of some of the novel's characters. Wenders's Therese is similar not only to the woman Wilhelm Meister proposed to, but also to some of the other women who beguiled him, such as Mariane, Philine, Aurelie, and Natalie. As well as Goethe's Laertes, Wenders's Laertes resembles the Harper in the novel. Bernhard combines elements of Wilhelm Meister's artistic colleagues, Melina and Serlo. The Industrialist is a dark parody of Jarno in his castle. Only the character of Mignon stays virtually constant: in the film, she remains an androgynous, mysterious girl who has a powerful love for Wilhelm of an ambiguously filial and erotic nature. Even with these variations, however, the characters play the same elementary function in both the novel and the film; this is a third point of comparison between the works. Engaging with them, Wilhelm Meister and Wilhelm are each drawn into an episodic comedy of errors.

It is in how their chain of blunders eventually form stories that the novel and the film sharply diverge. In Goethe's work, Wilhelm Meister's wanderings and misjudgments are eventually unified into a story of an education, of how the protagonist found his true place in society—which turns out not to be that of an artist after all. In Wenders's work, Wilhelm's movements are not only wrong; they are *falsche*—that is, not real movements at all. His travel fails to make any significant difference to him and the film stresses this with its absurdist tone. This lack of formative change, which destroys his relationships before they develop, which is perpetuated by his incorrigible unconnectedness to people and the world, makes the film a story about an education that does not take place. By emphasizing its absence, Wenders seconds Goethe's insight that the events that move us, even when they lead us to pursue tangents that provoke further course corrections when they are retrospectively regarded as errors, may in the end add up to a whole and meaningful life path. When they do not, something beyond a youthful course of errors has gone manifestly and humorously amiss.

The meaning of this divergence between the novel's and the film's stories, however, is complicated and deepened by the different formal qualities of the *Bildungsroman* and Wenders road movie genres. Again, an exhaustive comparison is beyond the scope of this brief discussion, but I want to zero in on a point at stake in my final observation of the last paragraph. With its happy and redemptive ending, Goethe's novel tells Wilhelm Meister's education story from a point of view at its end. Education here is the product of a conclusive review of a youthful period of life: now that Wilhelm Meister has successfully realized the point of his travels, how they changed him into a definite person ready to take up a particular social station, his education is over. In contrast, Wenders's Wilhelm is still erring. This may be due not only to problems in his character, though; it may also be shaped by the distinctive nature of cinema. As I observed in my discussion of *Alice*, because film is essentially a recording medium, it is at bottom rooted in the present tense: it registers not someone's memories or imagination, but something that is actually happening. Since such occurrences are always provisional and ongoing, a film rings most true, then, when it shows us something that is open-ended. For this reason, it makes sense that as a creature of cinema, Wilhelm can only be still in the process of being educated. Unlike in the *Bildungsroman*, he can never reach the end of the process—this is vital for what education means for Wenders.

Indeed, it is merely something like a gestalt switch that separates a Wilhelm preoccupied with and repeating his wrong moves, from one affirming his educative destiny. This becomes clear in a couple of exchanges with Therese. As he strolls with her on the Rhine, Wilhelm explains that he has a special, "erotic view" on things he has missed: he not only sees what he has overlooked but this sight moves him. Accordingly, when at the end of the film he declares that he has decided to part from her, he adds, "I know I shall love you very much one day." It is no surprise, then, that as he stands atop the Zugspitze, the very image of the romantic hero in Caspar David Friedrich's painting *Wanderer above the Sea of Fog*, he is filled not with a feeling of cosmic transcendence, but with regret for what he did not realize about her (Figure 3.8). But there is a way in which this erotic view could move him very differently. Suppose he were to notice, instead, that what he has missed, what he recurrently misses, is something that comes into his life which he takes for granted. After all, Wilhelm is a native of Glückstadt, which may also be translated as "Luck City." If he appreciated more understandingly the constant granting of grace in his life, made visible in his uncanny magnetism, he would be less tempted to pity himself. He might be, instead, inspired to write by the world present.

That this does not happen, that Wilhelm fails so far to realize his destiny, that he continues to want to write instead of writing devotedly, makes *Wrong Move*,

Figure 3.8 *Wrong Move* directed by Wim Wenders © Solaris Film, Munich/Westdeutscher Rundfunk, Cologne 1975. All rights reserved.

despite its depiction of endless travel, an anti-road-movie. What is essentially missing is the education that alters someone. By his amusing yet affectionate criticism of Wilhelm's blindness, Wenders reinforces the sense that for him, the road movie genre must call for its protagonist to be led out not only in physical space, but also in inner understanding. For Wilhelm's story to turn out right, he would have to turn into a person who affirms the path he has been moving on by his next move. In the cinematic world that is always still appearing, though, this can still happen, just around the bend.

* * *

This chapter has tried to strengthen our grasp of the Wenders road movie by examining how its core family features compare with similar ones in neighboring genres. In particular, I have focused on the themes of travel, destiny, and education. They help define what this specific genre of film both is and is not. In the next chapter, I shall pursue further Wenders's interest in education. As he elaborates in additional films more examples of what it may look like, he also elucidates its basic form. Someone's education, someone's experience of being led out, may be understood and represented as a figurative journey. Conversely, the concrete journeys depicted in Wenders's road movies may be also understood to be figures of particular educations. These pictures are thus ripe for recategorization.

4

Education Movies

I have been making the case that the voyages in Wenders's road movies have a decidedly educational meaning for their protagonists. Their travels transform them. In this chapter, I would like to shift this argument's emphasis slightly. I want to explore how an additional group of Wenders's films that are not centered on road trips, but which do concern a protagonist's education, portray that education as a kind of journey. In these pictures, we watch this person become someone who is distinctly not the same as he or she was at the beginning. This alteration takes the form of a gradual realization on the person's part that his or her life as a whole is being led out. It has been responding in a particular way that can be followed through on to the four questions of destiny. Even if this character is not marked by the experience of long-distance travel, then, his or her educational travel is shown to make a life-defining difference.

Four films of Wenders portray these journeys in especially moving ways: *Wings of Desire*, *Palermo Shooting*, *The Salt of the Earth*, and *Every Thing Will Be Fine*. As in Chapter 3, I shall take up these films one by one in chronological order. I remain interested in how the director's work and interests develop over the course of his career. Indeed, it is intriguing that three of the pictures on this list come after, and perhaps mutate out of, his last work to date in the road movie genre, *Don't Come Knocking*. Another way I follow the example of my third chapter is that my examination of the films is alert to comparisons. Once again, I want to discern how the films build on and depart from their precursors, thus opening up a field of variations on a set of common concerns and conventions. It is my hope that this might invite further exploration of the education movie genre. Finally, like the earlier chapters, my focus is more on the films' stories than their imagery or music. It is in them that their education lies.

To be clear, I should note that Wenders has never employed the term *education movie* to describe these or other works. The designation is a coinage of mine. Furthermore, I acknowledge that were a casual reader to come across this label, he or she would probably take it to refer to a movie about someone's experiences in school. We can think of plenty of films that feature dramas among students and teachers, set in classrooms, corridors, and schoolyards. I want the term to draw our attention to something separate from our activities of learning, however. My argument in this chapter is that the following films of Wenders show us what education without learning may look like. In the next chapter, I shall discuss more fully why our prevailing emphasis on learning actually threatens our education.

* * *

Wings of Desire is probably Wenders's most famous work. It came out in 1987, on the heels of *Paris, Texas* and *Tokyo-ga*. The German title, *Der Himmel über Berlin* (The Sky over Berlin), telegraphs the fact that even more than its forerunners, this film is rooted in a single place. At the center of its story, which was co-written with Handke, is a plain old romance, but one enhanced by an outlandish metaphor. The male protagonist is an angel who dwells in the heavens. He falls in love with a woman trapezist who lives in the city.

The angel is named Damiel. The film's opening sequence of shots places him in relation to us: the first is a shot of the sky; the next, of an eye in the sky; next, of the city viewed from above; next, of him standing on the Gedächtniskirche tower looking down; and next, of a mass of pedestrians crossing a road below, with a lone girl standing in the middle of the intersection looking up. With these few strokes, Wenders postulates that just as our wondering and longing view of the sky belongs to viewers who are earthbound, so a reverse-angle view of these earthly humans, one which is equally wondering and longing, would by implication belong to a skybound, angelic viewer. Such a being can only be sensed by children, though. The film gathers us, presumably childlike viewers, then, and follows Damiel as he moves about the metropolis, occasionally becoming visible to us in glimpses. We listen with him to the inner voices of people he momentarily visits as they go about their lives, oblivious to his presence. This activity of his is left unexplained until we shortly arrive at a scene in which Damiel finally speaks, to his angel friend, Cassiel.

The two of them are sitting in the front seats of a sporty convertible. Unlike the various cars in which Wenders's road movie characters travel, however, this one turns out to be a stationary model on display in a store. This visual jibe aside, Damiel and Cassiel's roving similarly inspires conversation, one which starts off being about their work and becomes one about their discontent (Figure 4.1).

From their talk, we comprehend that to be an angel is to participate in a vast, collective work of recording. What Damiel, Cassiel, and their colleagues are registering for eternity is every instance of human consciousness and thinking, of *Geist* (spirit). Mirroring in modernist fashion the very medium by which they are here depicted, the angels resemble, in this sense, a black-and-white camera and microphone that moves from person to person throughout the metropolis, lingering to attend lovingly to a few moments of someone's activity and inner monologue. They fly about on their recording rounds like bees gathering pollen to produce honey. Or, to switch metaphors, they seem to be translating the temporal world of human thinking into Baruch Spinoza's eternal world of God's ideas.[1] Conversely, the film they generate ends up largely taking the form of an accumulation of shots of various men, women, and children haphazardly engaged in these thoughtful activities; these

Figure 4.1 *Wings of Desire* directed by Wim Wenders © Road Movies Filmproduktion, Berlin/Argos Films, Paris/Westdeutscher Rundfunk, Cologne 1987. All rights reserved.

---

[1] See Baruch Spinoza, *Ethics*, in *The Collected Works of Spinoza, Volume I*, ed. and trans. Edwin Curley (Princeton: Princeton University Press, 1985).

mini-vignettes regularly interrupt the central story and give *Wings* much of its distinctive, disjunctive look. As in the past, Wenders stresses the episodic nature of experience; his collage of such experiences amounts to a portrait of urban life. This focus on the fleeting suchness of every moment of spirit furthermore suggests that the reason the angels can be perceived only by kids is because the latter still have the capacity to marvel at all the diverse forms of the world, at how each thing appears as this and not as that—the angels appear to be moved by this wonder to an inexhaustible degree. In this respect, a youthful being like Alice Van Dam in Wenders's original road movie, watching a bird fly between the skyscrapers, approaches the angelic condition. Damiel and Cassiel are conversing in the car, then, so that they can share every little comparable delight they have found in this city of human thinking. Later, we see that they and the rest of the angels are accordingly drawn to make their hive Berlin's central library.

As their dialogue continues, though, it becomes clear that Damiel and Cassiel also look at the human world with a certain longing. They know that a person is a bodily as well as a spiritual being, but they cannot experience physical sensation. They can mimic certain actions, such as picking up a pen, but like someone who merely thinks about picking up a pen, the material touch of the thing eludes them. Indeed, this world's emotional coloring is also invisible to them; hence the black-and-white nature of the film. Because of this limitation, their infinite interest in human thinking is bound to make them curious about human feeling too. They cannot help but wonder, with a touch of envy, about what it would be like to live and be engrossed in the physical world.

Despite their invisibility and the ontological gap that separates them from us, the angels do occasionally have an effect on those they watch over. As Wenders shows, we all tend to go through the motions of our lives absorbed in worry. On occasion, though, we may respond to an angel's presence with a surge of well-being. Perhaps this is because in the midst of weariness, pain, and confusion, the touch of one can recall a person to a sense of clarity and delight. As we may remember, Alice had this effect on Phillip Winter. Even as we near death, as in the case of a motorcycle accident victim depicted in *Wings*, we may wonder one last time at all the forms we share the world with.

After Damiel and Cassiel conclude their conversation and spend some time with their colleagues in the library, they separate and resume their rounds.

Damiel's takes him to a circus tent where he watches the trapeze artist, Marion, practice her number garbed in a mock pair of wings. The rehearsal comes to a halt when the manager suddenly shows up and announces that the circus will close after the evening's show because the money has run out. A wave of sharp disappointment hits Marion, registered in her thoughts; she is then engulfed by numb emptiness laced with superstitious fear that the full moon on her last night means that she is doomed to fall. As she struggles with these emotions, she begins to consider her life as a whole. Who is she if not a trapezist? How should she live now? She feels like a stranger in the world. Leaving the main circus ring, she walks to her home; like the car in the store, it is a trailer that is only temporarily at rest. Damiel follows her.

After being initially bemused by Marion's angel impersonation, what captivates him appears to be the very unangelic pathos of her reflections on her life. At one point, Marion exclaims in her inner soliloquy, "desire to love!" and the film image blossoms for an instant into color. It is as if Marion's fear of death and need to live meaningfully flare into a hunger to love something, and this longing momentarily moves Damiel, humanizing him. He begins to realize that she has the power to introduce him to the things of the heart.

In the meantime, Cassiel accompanies an elderly storyteller named, fittingly, Homer, who also rambles around the city. This Homer too wants to weave an epic, but one of not war but peace. Such a visionary exercise, he believes, has the power to shield people from current troubles and protect them for the future. In it, "the onions that are drying" are just as precious as "the tree trunk that traverses a swamp." Every happening is on a par with every other, and does not conflict with anything in this world without heroes and kings. Each one, pursued in story, may fuel and keep aflame the imagination of an all-encompassing harmony. Homer acknowledges to himself that he is a near-invisible, *poète maudit*; he has faith, however, that this epic form holds the key to his and his readers' common bond.[2] "If humanity ever lost its storyteller," he muses, "it would lose its childhood," its angelic awareness. Yet, as Cassiel listens to him, the angel appears to grasp ruefully that this kind of narration is nothing like the archiving of facts.

---

[2] Handke discusses this concept of the epic throughout Peter Handke and Peter Hamm, *Vive les illusions! Entretiens*, trans. Anne Weber (Paris: Christian Bourgeois, 2008).

Moreover, in contrast to the idea of peace as the imagination of the harmonious happening of the world, *Wings* suggests that war is something like a grandiosely produced, unnatural spectacle. It does this by having Cassiel and Damiel rendezvous again at the shooting site of a movie about the Second World War. We watch a large film crew busily staging and choreographing its scenes, fighting against the expensively ticking clock. As they fuss on the enormous set with its fancy props and equipment, the patiently waiting actors chat and play pinball, dressed in the costumes of victims and victimizers. One of them is Peter Falk, playing himself, the ubiquitously recognizable star of the television show, *Columbo*. His running monologue comments with humorous irony on Wenders's usual bête noire, the image industry. It turns out that Peter Falk is a former angel; later, he will give Damiel encouragement when the latter likewise makes the switch to being human. Before that, and after drinking in the majestic movie set, however, Damiel leads Cassiel away to show him a much more modest, child-oriented festival, the circus act.

After watching the first part together, Cassiel leaves and Damiel concentrates again on Marion who fascinates him. During the intermission, he listens to her wrestle with her fear of death in her trailer and then watches her pull herself together and perform her angel act in the heights. After she pulls it off, she is filled with a sense of relief, well-being, and a readiness to start her life over again. This inspires her that night to dream in her sleep of her angel, the one who would stay close and care for her. As if in response, then, Damiel tells Cassiel that he is going to join her. Shortly after her last night on the trapeze for now, he decides to make the transition to being earthbound.

When he falls from the heavens, Damiel enters into our Oz-world of colors. After tasting some of its sensations, including the overwhelming one of heartbreak when he finds the site of the circus deserted, he eventually succeeds in locating Marion at a rock concert. While Nick Cave and the Bad Seeds play "From Her to Eternity" in the auditorium next door, he and she meet face to face at last in the club's empty bar.

Their encounter is mythically staged, elucidating an idea of marriage. Damiel is dressed in a suit, Marion in a red dress. He is silent throughout their meeting; at the start, he offers her a drink of wine; at the end, he leans his head on hers and then kisses and embraces her. In the middle, he listens intently as she discloses herself to him in an intoxicated, poetic speech. She explains that what she wants now is to live seriously. Before, she was sometimes alone, sometimes with others; either way, her life was determined by chance and caprice and felt directionless. At present, she is ready to commit herself decisively to an "image of necessity" in a partner's eyes (Figure 4.2). She will love someone who needs her; she will affirm in turn her need to be this specific person's lover. And if this necessary life is something he reciprocally decides to join her in, if it is something that he is inspired to give himself to, equally, then their wedding would exemplify the life of the people. Their mutual commitment would reproduce the symbolic act that brings together a community and their children would reproduce its generations.

At the end, then, Marion and Damiel together commence their destiny. "There is no greater story than ours," claims Marion, "that of man and woman." Cassiel watches them from a melancholy distance, only half understanding. And just as Phillip Winter found guidance for his storytelling in John Ford, Homer calls on the couple to tell theirs as an epic of peace. In it, Damiel has changed from being a lover of spirit to a particular woman's lover. Marion has changed from a whimsical being of fortune into someone who is seriously committed to a partner in necessity. These transformations are the result of an educational journey, one that never leaves Berlin.

Who is being led out? On the one hand, it is Damiel, someone who finds that his life as a whole is unfeeling, and on the other, Marion, someone who finds that her life is arbitrary.

Figure 4.2 *Wings of Desire* directed by Wim Wenders © Road Movies Filmproduktion, Berlin/Argos Films, Paris/Westdeutscher Rundfunk, Cologne 1987. All rights reserved.

From where are they led? They are drawn away from the realms of eternity and luck.

To where are they led? They are drawn to a shared destiny.

What leads them out? Their encounter sustained by their marriage and by Homer's epic form.

As a postscript to this discussion, let me mention that *Wings* was followed in 1993 by a quasi-sequel, *Faraway, So Close!* This film features many of the earlier characters, notably Damiel, Marion, Peter Falk, and Cassiel. It focuses this time on Cassiel's journey from being an angel to becoming human to becoming an angel again. It depicts how he responds to the challenges of living as a human and how these responses involve him with a growing network of people and their conflicts. The film articulates a number of thought-provoking insights into the human condition and it does this within the framework of an engaging story. But I do not consider it one of Wenders's education movies.

The reason is that in my judgment, Cassiel's story does not ultimately lead him out anywhere. Despite his miraculous, ontological metamorphoses from angel to human to angel, and despite his more mundane history of gradually adapting to the ways of the human world, his fundamental character never alters. In particular, it is not led from one defining configuration of concerns to a quite different one. At the end of the film, Cassiel sacrifices his life for another; in this, he echoes the culminating devotional acts of many of Wenders's protagonists. The only sticking point, from the perspective of this essay, is that no personal conversion appears to bring him to this sacrifice. Unlike Damiel who commits his old being to the new destiny he is weaving with Marion in *Wings*, Cassiel in *Faraway* seems never to have forgotten, or truly lost, his original nature. He is a kind of angelic brother of the more foolishly obtuse Wilhelm in *Wrong Move*.

* * *

With *Palermo Shooting*, we jump closer to Wenders's most recent work. He released this film in 2008. It concerns a breakdown experienced by a photographer named Finn. After his crisis is resolved, this man has become a different person and the change has less to do with his trip to the title city than with an interior journey.

That education commences one night when Finn is driving home from a party. With the top of his convertible down, he reaches for his camera with one hand and lifts it above the windshield in order to take a panoramic photo of his surroundings, all the while steering the car with his other hand. He has performed this intricate maneuver before, but this time, he momentarily loses control of the vehicle and it swerves into the adjoining lane of incoming traffic. In a miraculous stroke of luck, he manages simultaneously to avoid crashing into a car and to snap a picture of that car's occupant. Totally shaken, Finn pulls off the road, abandons his automobile, and begins walking.

The streets he wanders through belong to Düsseldorf, where Finn is leading a life full of accolades, glamour, and pleasure. His work is celebrated in museums around the world. His services are sought after by rich clients: at one point, on a cheesy stage featuring a factory, a little red boat, and a flying saucer, we watch him do a fashion shoot of the pregnant celebrity model Milla Jovovich, playing herself. While his products receive their finishing touches from a team of assistants in a hyper-stylish studio, he delivers lectures on his art at a university. In the evenings, he is swarmed at chic gallery parties. He is in the process of separating from an old girlfriend and of stringing along a new one. All in all, he is the very image of success, resembling the photographer protagonist of Michelangelo Antonioni's film *Blow-Up*.[3]

But Finn is not only generally discontented; he also has a particular problem about time. With so much to do and enjoy, he lives at a hurtling pace, never pausing to savor anything. Unsurprisingly, then, he also experiences this time as endless stasis; when he looks out of his window, he sees a dreary city that never changes. Perhaps to compensate for this ennui, he makes a career of constructing landscape photos out of different places blended together using digital manipulation. Replying to criticism from one of his students that this work is ultimately unphotographic, he denies that there is anything to a photo except its produced surface. Still, his restlessness seems to belie this expression of self-satisfaction. He acts not like someone who is sure of himself but like one who is in a race he is losing. Moreover, his being perpetually on the go is aggravated by the fact that he is unable to sleep at night except in snatches. As soon as he drops off, he recurrently dreams of the approach of death and of his deceased mother whom he misses; these nightmares jolt him awake.

---

[3] Wenders acknowledges the influence of *Blow-Up* and Ingmar Bergman's *The Seventh Seal* on *Palermo Shooting* in Wim Wenders, "On 30 July 2007: INGMAR BERGMAN AND MICHELANGELO ANTONIONI," in *The Pixels of Paul Cézanne and Reflections on Other Artists* (London: Faber and Faber, 2018).

In a sense, Finn's brush with fate on the road amounts to the opening invasion of these dreams into his waking world. Even as a literal collision is avoided, the frightening and despairing imagery of his nightmares (which in their style resemble some of Ingmar Bergman's films) enters the world of things and people around him. The car that almost killed him seems sent from the same place as the unhappiness he is running away from and haunted by. Shortly after the near crash, he imagines himself a corpse in the wreckage. This is his initial picture of death (Figure 4.3). Then, as he walks on, he realizes that he feels dead and yearns, as many of Wenders's characters do, for his whole life to change.

Finn ends up sleeping for a bit that night in a tree at a park. When the morning sun awakens him, he notices that he is surrounded by sheep. He chats with the man herding them who explains he enjoys doing this work because it allows him to relish time's slow passage. Even before they have talked much, the shepherd looks understandingly and compassionately at him and gently advises him to perform every action as if it were for the last time. Perhaps because Finn is so taken by this uncannily prophetic conversation, when the shepherd directs his attention to a boat sailing down the Rhine, which bears the name *Palermo*, he spontaneously decides to travel to that place. Returning home, he persuades Milla Jovovich—who had earlier expressed a wish that the camera would do better justice to her childbearing state—his manager, and a small crew to redo the shoot in a less bombastic, more intimate setting over there.

Figure 4.3 *Palermo Shooting* directed by Wim Wenders © Neue Road Movies/Arte France Cinéma/Zweites Deutsches Fernsehen 2008. All rights reserved.

After the Palermo shooting turns out well, everyone departs the city except Finn. Improvising on his earlier decision, he stays on and takes a moratorium from work. As at Düsseldorf, he resumes walking the streets, sometimes taking photos of things that happen to catch his eye. These shots of naturally happening life powerfully recall those that graced *Alice* and *Lisbon Story* in the past. But because it is Finn's perambulations, and not the barely depicted plane flight to the Italian town, that play a central role in his story, I am reluctant to call this more recent film a road movie.

As Finn wanders for several days in Palermo's street maze, two things change in him that tighten the tie between his dreams and his feelings. First, he becomes increasingly despondent about his life. One night, he breaks down weeping in the middle of a drinking bout; the next day, he confides to a fellow photographer he meets that he is at a complete loss. The second change is that he more frequently dozes off in public places and plunges into nightmares. When he wakes up this time, however, he sees an archer shooting at him; he even perceives the arrows narrowly missing him, before they vanish. Instead of discounting these visions as some kind of hallucinatory malady, he becomes preoccupied with them as absolutely real. He starts to believe that he is being hunted.

One morning, as Finn awakens from one of these nightmares on a bench in a crumbling theater house, he finds himself being sketched by a woman, Flavia. Although he wants to pursue a conversation with her, she quits him rather coolly. Later that day, after falling asleep yet again on a hilltop and dreaming of the archer, he sits up with a start and experiences his camera being knocked out of his hand and damaged by an arrow. He runs into Flavia again at a museum, where she is working to restore a painting, and tells her that a mysterious archer whose face he cannot see has been pursuing him. Surprisingly, she is quite interested; she takes a break and they go to a quay to talk. In the middle of their conversation, he suddenly spots his stalker. As he tries to point the figure out to her, he is hit by an arrow and tumbles into the water, losing his camera altogether. Despite not knowing how to swim, he manages to rise to the light and is rescued and revived by Flavia. She takes him to her home to recover before returning to work.

Finn rejoins Flavia at the museum where she shows him the painting she is repairing. It is entitled *The Triumph of Death* and pictures a commanding, skeletal rider on horseback shooting transparent arrows at the townspeople below. Flavia explains that the most challenging and crucial part of the puzzle is getting the face of the archer right. She additionally shares with Finn her own brush with mortality: she recently lost her boyfriend when he fell from a scaffold doing the same work as hers. Because she is still haunted by the senselessness of him being taken from her, and because Finn's experiences echo her anguish and the image she is trying to reconstruct, she recognizes that they have a bond. Perhaps together they can reach a better understanding of the approach of death.

Flavia decides to transport Finn out of Palermo to a hopefully safer place in the town of Gangi. There, she has a house, passed down to her by her grandmother, to which she returns whenever she needs sanctuary and solace. This echo of *Alice* is compounded by one of *Kings*: Flavia leaves him for a bit and returns at first to the house alone, where she weeps over its ruin and her memories. It is in the old family home of his conversational partner, then, that Finn has his final, revelatory dream.

In it, a figure recognized to be Death welcomes him to an old library and announces that his name is about to be entered into its archive. (Not only does Death so personified bring back memories of Bergman's 1957 film *The Seventh Seal*, the actor playing Death in *Palermo Shooting*, Dennis Hopper, also played Tom, the American friend *fatal*, in Wenders's 1977 noir.) Terrified, Finn tries to escape, to no avail. "I love my life!" he protests. Death insists to the contrary that he did not demonstrate any such love and points to his practice of embellishing and illusorily recreating "life" in his images. His fear of death is misplaced fear of real, passing life, of how it takes part of us as it slips away. But there is another way to look at this. When one embraces death, particularly in photographically stilled life, one affirms that death is a condition for the world, things, and people being precious to us. Death is "the opening, the connecting door, the only way out" that leads from self-possessiveness to love. This realization transforms Finn. He gives himself to Death, accepts from Death his restored camera, and prepares to take a picture of Death. The character with Hopper's smiling, seductive features metamorphoses into a figure to be found in many of Wenders's films: the beloved mother (Figure 4.4).

When Finn awakens, he recalls in memory images the story of how he arrived at this place. This destiny puts him at peace with time. He turns toward Flavia, who opens her eyes and addresses to him the word "you." In her face, at the film's close, he sees our common mortality.

Figure 4.4 *Palermo Shooting* directed by Wim Wenders © Neue Road Movies/Arte France Cinéma/Zweites Deutsches Fernsehen 2008. All rights reserved.

What does it mean to photograph death? At the start of Finn's crisis, it is to glimpse what he is most terrified of: that his accelerating pace of life will lead him to lose it. This picture develops out of his unhappy nightmares and then takes on substance in the world as a force that is attacking him. Wenders personifies this force, following the Palermo painting, as a fearsome archer. Less dramatically, it is not uncommon for such forces, repressed from consciousness but haunting one's dreams, to manifest themselves as neurotic symptoms, such as having one's body suddenly and uncontrollably jerk as if it had been hit by an arrow. In any case, things turn around for Finn, in a fashion characteristic of Wenders, when he is found by Flavia and they fall into dialogue. Her similar experiences and sympathy, and her knowledge of the painting, enable her to help him understand and elaborate the visual language of his anxieties. Indeed, in his concluding dream in her company, he makes the connection between his imagery of death and his photography; this dispels his fear and transforms him into a different person. Death is not a horrifying figure hunting him. It is a loving one that calls him, that inspires his vocation. He realizes that whenever he sees something dear in the world that moves him to preserve its memory in an image, that sentiment is a present of death. His photographic work, then, could be more deliberately devoted to honoring this maternal source of beauty.

Who is being led out? Finn, a photographer at odds with the temporal passing of his life.

From what is he led? He is drawn away from his fear of death.

To where is he led? He is drawn to an appreciation of how death makes it possible for him to love things and people in the world.

What leads him out? Two things, it appears to me. First, there is Flavia, who draws him into a therapeutic conversation that enables him to face and better understand what he is afraid of. And then there is the city of Palermo, which inspires him to devote himself to a more loving approach to photography. His responsiveness to the world is rekindled by the mortal beauty of Palermo's street life, in which he makes himself at home.

* * *

In 2014, Wenders released another film about a photographer, *The Salt of the Earth*. He co-directed this feature with Juliano Ribeiro Salgado and it focuses on the renowned work of the latter's father, Sebastião Salgado. Like *Palermo Shooting*, the story is centered on a man whose encounters with death throw his life into crisis. Sebastião finds himself at a point where he despairs of his work because his soul has been sickened. As in the earlier film, a kind of grace saves him, however, and he ends up reaffirming and pursuing in a revised direction his photographic calling.

Unlike Wenders's other education or road movies, this film is nonfictional. It returns us to a question I discussed in the previous chapter: Why do road movie stories about travel and destiny lend themselves to fiction? In response, I argued that such stories appeal to their audience members' latent interest in reflecting on their own destinies; this rhetorical function of theirs favors an emphasis on dramatic imagination. The more movingly the film can stage a story that evokes the kind of soul-searching natural to situations of serious internal conflict, the more likely the viewer will be to ponder and question his or her own subjective experiences in analogous situations. In contrast, a documentary's characteristic interest in establishing objective facts about the world is liable to steer it away from such visionary exercises.

The Salt of the Earth, in my judgment, is a stunning exception to this rule. It is, indeed, devoted to documenting and discussing the diverse subjects of Sebastião's photography. These exotic people (to most Western gallery and book audiences) and their situations are what this film is chiefly about. As a way of examining them in sequence, the film places Sebastião's encounters with them, which he registered in photos, in the context of his career's history. Its employment of this form makes the film a typical work of cinematic nonfiction. What gives it an unusual, educational force, though, is Wenders's and Juliano Salgado's decision to appoint Sebastião the principal narrator of this history. He is a gripping first-person storyteller. His words, in combination with the piercing images from his camera, pull us into what it feels like to accompany these people and provoke us to reflect on what it means that each of us too shares the planet with them. His stories and pictures end up providing the film with dramatic and imaginative resources that are the equal of any in its fictional cousins.

Salt's opening demonstrates the power of this combination. Sebastião discusses some of his pictures of gold miners at work; he elaborates on their Serra Pelada setting and on what he witnessed and thought about as he explored this sublime and teeming cavity in the earth. Shortly after this introduction to him, the film takes us to a spot in the mountains near his Brazilian hometown of Aimorés to which his father used to take him; there, he talks about the emergence of a boyhood desire to travel and see the world. We are then accordingly transported to a remote jungle in West Papua where the adult man photographs a tribal ceremony. How did the Brazilian boy become the accomplished, fearless, and trusted cosmopolitan photographer he is today? This question, set up in the three episodes above, establishes the direction of the film's central story. The latter ends up being about how the various strangers he met profoundly changed him.

It begins with Sebastião leaving his birthplace for the city of Vitoria where he attends high school and college. He studies economics and prepares to make that his profession. It is there that he also meets and marries his lifelong spouse, Lélia. In the sixties, the two of them become involved in left-wing political agitation and after the military consolidates its rule over the country, they flee Brazil in 1969 for Paris. Sebastião finds himself there increasingly enamored of photography and with Lélia's support, he decides to abandon his career as an economist and devote his life to it. The two of them travel to Niger in 1973 and he begins his new work concentrating on undeveloped, non-Western communities.

Shortly afterward, they have their son Juliano. While Lélia raises him and pursues her own work as an architect, Sebastião undertakes his first major collection, *Other Americas*, which gathers photos taken between 1977 and

1984.[4] These come from a series of visits to secluded, indigenous and peasant communities in Latin America. As a selection of these images is presented in *Salt*, Sebastião focuses his voiceover narration on the distinctive ways of life these peoples fashioned for themselves. While sharing with us this anthropological passion, he occasionally also avers that these visits made a deep impression on him personally. It is fair to say that these records of his travels place this film close to Wenders's road movies. The reason I demur from considering it an example of that genre is that the imagery and narration for the most part concern Sebastião's observations about these communities, and not his voyages to these places.

In 1979, the Salgado family is enlarged by the birth of Rodrigo, who struggles with Down syndrome. Around the same time, Brazil's military government declares an amnesty for political dissidents and the Salgados return to their native country for the first time in a decade. From 1981 to 1983, Sebastião travels through Northeastern Brazil and photographs peasant communities in that area. The suffering he sees changes him and makes him rethink what it means to be a photographer. In the meantime, coming home to his family farm run by his aging parents, he discovers that it is dying from a prolonged drought.

Sebastião's new direction in photography manifests itself in a collection of work done between 1984 and 1986 entitled *Sahel: The End of the Road*.[5] Traveling with members of Doctors without Borders through desperate, malnourished, and plague-stricken camps in this African region, he dedicates himself to bearing witness to preventable human misery and death, devastation that is allowed to happen because of political greed and corruption. "I really wanted . . . to show that a large part of humanity was suffering from great distress due to a problem of sharing and not just a natural disaster." His testimony is heartbreaking and conscience-searing. Pursuing this calling further, he turns to *Workers*, a project that occupies him from 1986 to 1991.[6] This collection examines the job and living conditions of diverse laborers all over the world. On their bodies for all to see are the marks of their exhaustion, malnutrition, and exposure to mechanical danger and the elements. Finally, in 1993, he

---

[4] See Sebastião Salgado, *Other Americas* (New York: Pantheon Books, 1986).
[5] See Sebastião Salgado, *Sahel: The End of the Road* (Berkeley: University of California Press, 2004).
[6] See Sebastião Salgado, *Workers: An Archaeology of the Industrial Age* (New York: Aperture, 1993).

begins to compose *Exodus*, which records the plights of masses of refugees around the globe.[7] This project lasts until 1999 and represents the crescendo of his portraits of suffering.

Most of the people Sebastião photographed in *Exodus* were fleeing war and persecution in places such as Tanzania, Congo, and Yugoslavia. His camera documents the enormous, impersonal scale of the cruelty and slaughter that was inflicted on these very individual beings, and the mass reduction of their humanity to the most desperate and wretched state. In one of the images, a mother communes with a child in the middle of the devastation (Figure 4.5). One can hardly bear to see many of these photos and he speaks painfully about his horror in taking them. Finally, while covering the succession of Rwandan massacres on both sides, he is crippled in body and soul. Having witnessed such human barbarity, he reaches a point where he no longer believes in anything, in any redemption for our species. "We didn't deserve to live. No one deserved to live." His trip into our heart of darkness leads him to doubt that any of his work has meaning.

Figure 4.5 *The Salt of the Earth* directed by Wim Wenders © Decia Films/Amazonas Images/Solares Fondazione delle Arti 2014. All rights reserved.

[7] See Sebastião Salgado, *Exodus* (Cologne: Taschen, 2016).

Meanwhile, the condition of the Salgado homestead worsens. Even as Sebastião despairs of his calling, Lélia galvanizes him to join her in a massive project to replant the forest surrounding the farm. After ten years of effort, their struggle bears fruit. Not only the trees, but a whole, healthy, sustainable ecosystem returns. Their surprising success leads to the formation of the Instituto Terra, dedicated to expanding environmental restoration and education.

It also leads to a revival of Sebastião's photography. Inspired by a new appreciation of nature's precious beauty and governing power, he realizes his work is being led in a different direction. He begins a project titled *Genesis*.[8] For the first time, he devotes himself to recording animals in habitats that have been for the most part undisturbed by humans (Figure 4.6). When he does return to human subjects, particularly those in virtually prehistoric communities, he depicts them as just another beast drawing on nature for sustenance. His epic of peace, so to speak, celebrates the nourishing and harmonizing power of the planet's ecosystem and expresses visionary confidence that in turn, for our

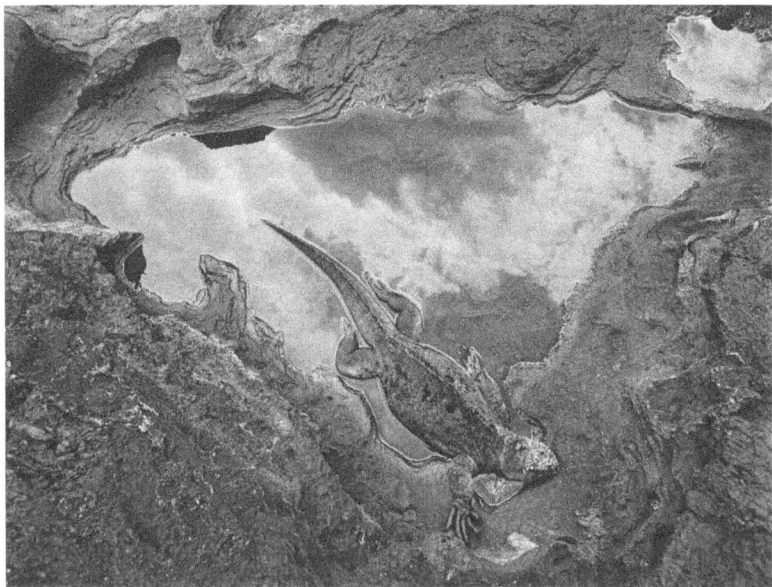

Figure 4.6 *The Salt of the Earth* directed by Wim Wenders © Decia Films/Amazonas Images/Solares Fondazione delle Arti 2014. All rights reserved.

---

[8] See Sebastião Salgado, *Genesis* (Cologne: Taschen, 2013).

part, we can help heal that ecosystem. "The destruction of the earth," he avows at the film's conclusion, "can be reversed."

In some ways, the photos Sebastião took of Nigerian tribespeople in 1973 are not all that unlike the contemporary ones he takes of their Zoé counterparts at the end of *Salt*. He has been consistently drawn to such premodern communities. But the regard with which he faced these people has developed over the course of his life. At the start, it was inspired by curiosity and a delight in otherness; later, by compassion and moral anguish; and after his dark night of the soul, during which it was unclear how he could go on with his vocation, by a love of the rule of nature. This change in him is expressed by his ability to tell a story about his life's path and destiny. Linking together his many photographic voyages and his tales of what he saw is thus an overarching, internal, educational journey. Imagining it may make a difference to our own.

Who is being led out? Sebastião, a photographer whose explorations of how very different communities live disclose to him a sickening propensity to callousness and evil that is in us all.

From where is he led? He is drawn away from an anthropocentric view of the world.

To where is he led? He is drawn to a nature-centric one that nourishes faith in the possibility that we may cooperate in the world's restoration.

What leads him out? It is his and Lélia's work replanting and caring for the forest around their family home.

*　*　*

The last work to be discussed is 2015's *Every Thing Will Be Fine*. At the core of this film is a story that takes place over a decade: a man gradually recovers from traumatic guilt over his part in a boy's accidental death. Unlike more conventional movies, there are virtually no pressing deadlines to be met, surprise plot twists, intense dramatic conflicts, or suspense-inducing moments of uncertainty or danger. Instead, we watch how the nature and progress of this man's inner healing is disclosed in a series of un-extraordinary events. Periodically, the picture jumps across a span of years; this enables it to show that the characters have become somewhat different people over this time. Like the other films in this chapter, this one is less about succeeding or failing to change the world to solve a problem, and more about educational change.

Before I delve into the story details, let me note one quality that distinguishes this picture from others in Wenders's oeuvre: its pronounced lyricism. The story rides on a symphonic score that is unusually prominent and pervasive. This music foregrounds the main characters' sentiments even when they are not bodily expressed or are even suppressed. In combination with this, Wenders builds on his experiments in the 2011 documentary *Pina*, and films in 3D. Unlike those who use this device to add punch to thrillers, he turns this cinematography into a language of contemplation. In 3D, his characters gain presence and the shifting spaces between them and other people and things become more palpable. So that viewers may dwell in this world of mood, distance, and connection, he draws us hypnotically into a story that is simpler, slower, and involves less physical action than many are used to.

It concerns Tomas, a writer living in Montreal. Not only is he struggling with his work, but his relationship with his girlfriend, Sara, is also floundering. One day, after a mediocre stint at his cabin desk and after sparring with Sara on the phone, he is diverted from his usual way home by a road closure. Driving in a snowstorm and momentarily distracted by Sara insistently calling his cellphone, he has only a second to slam on the brakes when he sees a kid toboggan right in his path. He barely misses hitting this boy, Christopher, and carries him to a nearby farmhouse and his mother, Kate. But they discover in horror that Tomas has run over and killed Kate's other son, Nicholas.

Brought home by the police, Tomas evades Sara's inquiries about what had happened and tells her that he desperately wants just to sleep. Starting the next day, the film begins to follow alternately Tomas's and Kate's lives, which have been linked together by this accident. Kate shovels snow and gathers firewood. Tomas too acts as if nothing has happened; he resumes his discussion with Sara about their relationship. But there is an edge to his complaints, suggesting he may harbor stifled anger about her disastrous phone call the previous evening.

The film skips ahead four months and discloses that the effects of the accident have intensified and breached the walls of the characters' routines. Tomas has separated from Sara. He tries to commit suicide in a motel room. While this is happening, Kate is in bed at the farmhouse in tears. While he recovers at a hospital, he is visited by Sara who has learned about what transpired not only at the motel but earlier in the road accident. She tries to reassure him that the boy's death was not his fault and he decides that he wants to try living with her again.

At the farmhouse sometime later, Kate is virtually paralyzed with grief. Tomas, on the other hand, starts writing again. He visits his elderly father who treats him with tyrannical disdain and bitterly complains about his loveless marriage, meaningless work, and wasted life. This appears to strengthen in Tomas a resolve not to become like him. Shortly afterward, Tomas's publisher tells Tomas that his work is markedly improving; he is also complimented by the publisher's colleague, Ann. As his work gains traction, though, his relationship with Sara runs into problems once more. He is glumly unenthusiastic about her plans for them to move into a new house. Meanwhile, Kate in despair turns to religion. She brings Christopher with her to church and prays, "I need help. I can't do this on my own." Although Tomas has found some footing for his work, both his and Kate's lives remain in free fall because of the disaster.

Two years pass. Tomas has published the novel he had started to write. The new episode in the film opens with him signing copies at a bookstore while his publisher and Ann look on, very pleased. As soon as he leaves the celebration, however, Tomas is compelled to drive back to the scene of the road accident where he encounters Kate for the first time since that night. Instead of lashing out, she welcomes his unexpected appearance and tells him, "We can only try to believe there is meaning to this." Moved by this reception, he jots down for her his name and phone number and declares, "It would make me feel a lot better if I could do something for you." Grasping his suffering, she has him wait a bit while she runs into the house and brings him a book. "Maybe this could help you." Although he demurs, saying he is not a believer, she presses him to take a look at it precisely as a favor to her.

Following this exchange of giving and receiving, Kate calls him up later in the evening. They chat for a while and she asks him to drive over again. When he arrives, she, in his company, ceremonially burns the novel she was absorbed in during the accident. She has been cursing herself for letting it cause her to be fatally inattentive. He reassures and comforts her as she pours out her own feelings of guilt (Figure 4.7). After they spend the night dozing on the couch, he leaves at sunrise. Their accidental, disastrous link has developed into something deeper.

Another four years pass. Tomas has broken up with Sara and embarked on a relationship with Ann. He has achieved a degree of public recognition for his writing, but it does not seem to gratify him much. Meanwhile, Kate appears happier at her chores and she reads with interest a newspaper story about him.

Figure 4.7 *Every Thing Will Be Fine* directed by Wim Wenders © Neue Road Movies/Montauk Productions/BAC Films Production/Göta Film/MER Film 2015. All rights reserved.

At an amusement park, Tomas and Ann announce to Ann's daughter, Mina, that they will all be moving in together into Tomas's house. As he did earlier with Sara, though, he displays some ambivalence about this plan. Suddenly, there is an accident and one of the cars falls off the Ferris wheel that they were just riding. In the midst of the panicking crowd, he responds coolly and practically, aiding one of the victims. Later at home, Ann expresses shock at his readiness to resume his writing routine as if nothing had happened. He compares his steady hands to her trembling ones and realizes she might be right that there is something wrong with him. His shutdown condition is perhaps dawning on him.

The film jumps ahead yet another four years. Tomas's once intimidating father has become senile and needy. After visiting him, Tomas attends a music performance with Ann; when he leaves the auditorium for a bit, he bumps into Sara. Unlike the similar, culminating scene in *Wings*, she tells him about how much he hurt her. When he clumsily tries to touch her, she strikes him and he runs away. Sometime after the concert, he receives a letter from Christopher. The boy, now sixteen, has been encouraged by the school psychologist to seek a meeting with him. Tomas sends an evasive reply but then Kate calls and impresses on him how much this would mean to Christopher. At their café meeting, then, Tomas insists to Christopher that it is pointless to dwell on the past. In response, the latter bursts out with agonized questions about why Tomas was so successful with his writing following the accident while his mother had found life so hard.

After some more months pass, Tomas and his family return one fall evening from a trip out of town to receive a literary award. He and Ann discover that someone has broken into the house and urinated in their bed. They report the incident to the police; subsequently, the shaken Ann and Mina leave to stay at Ann's parents' while Tomas remains behind to take care of the mess. Later, he sees the intruder lurking in the backyard. As if he already knows that it must be Christopher, he opens the door and waits for him to join him at the kitchen table. They talk through the night, with Christopher relaying news about his mother. In the morning, as Christopher is about to leave, Tomas suddenly reaches out and hugs him. He echoes Kate's welcoming reception of him years ago. Christopher bicycles off, elated. Tomas looks lovingly at a tree in the yard and weeps. In the film's last shot, he turns and smiles directly at the camera.

The deadly accident, then, transforms Tomas in stages. Prior to it, he was already struggling with his work and family; the accident throws his whole life into question. His initial reaction is to flee his feelings of guilt over his part in it. When he cannot escape through sleep, he tries to kill himself.

The aftermath of this leads to a second change in Tomas: he learns to detach himself from his emotional turmoil through writing. He develops a capacity to portray situations and experiences vividly as a perceptive spectator rather than an overwhelmed participant. This comes at a cost, however, in that he accordingly becomes less responsive to actual events and people around him. He distances himself not only from his guilt but also from Sara, whom he loses.

Things take yet another turn when Tomas and Kate share a moment of surprising closeness, recognizing and comforting each other's remorse. From this, he evidently draws the strength to start a new relationship with Ann. At first, it seems doomed to repeat some of the problems of the old one, but an echo of the road accident at the fair provides him with an opportunity to realize and work on his emotional unresponsiveness.

By the time Christopher reaches out to him four years later, Tomas has again changed. His view of his father is colored less by fear and resentment than by compassion. He can acknowledge his failings to Sara, although he still does not know how to rectify them with her. Similarly, although he is guarded about meeting Christopher and reluctant to reopen the old wound, he is no longer in headlong flight from it. When the repressed finally returns in the middle of the night, so to speak, he is able to receive Christopher with close to

Figure 4.8 *Every Thing Will Be Fine* directed by Wim Wenders © Neue Road Movies/Montauk Productions/BAC Films Production/Göta Film/MER Film 2015. All rights reserved.

the same empathy with which Kate had received him when he was drawn back to the accident scene. Indeed, his embrace the next morning of the brother of the boy he killed seconds her faith that the catastrophe can have a meaning. It can connect him to a family of shared suffering. Thus when Tomas looks at the tree, he sees what Finn in *Palermo* would call the face of death (Figure 4.8). And when he turns and smiles in the next shot, he is welcoming not only Ann and Mina who may be returning at that moment to the house, but also all of us who are a part of this mortal home. He has become someone who is ready to write out of attachment to the world.

Who is being led out? Tomas, a man who is struggling, after having accidentally killed a child, with the sense that he does not deserve to live.

From where is he led? He is drawn away from his defensive proneness to deaden himself to emotion.

To where is he led? He is drawn to accept that this disaster has connected him to others whom he loves.

Who leads him out? Kate and Christopher, his co-grieving family members.

* * *

These four films have their obvious differences. One of them is a work of nonfiction. Two employ rather fantastical elements while another stays close to ordinary, sorrowful life. The people and worlds that are pictured, the images and music that carry this depiction, vary as well. All of these features aside, though, the films resemble each other in the form of their stories.

At the story's center is a protagonist or protagonists who change. Although this transformation occurs at least in part in response to a particular problem, it involves coming to realize that such a challenge is an acceptable condition of life. Accordingly, Marion's desire to love, or Finn's fear that he is running out of time, or Sebastião's pain at needless suffering, are not rooted in things they succeed in eliminating. These characters eventually understand these problems to be part of a life that they each nevertheless affirm, even as they continue to struggle against them and some of the particular things in the world that make them worse.

How do they come to this affirmation? They do not do so all at once in some flash of insight. It takes Sebastião and Tomas, for example, years. Even the conversion of Finn must be traced back past his concluding dream to the sequence of events that leads up to it. The protagonists' changes have a history.

It is in how they make sense of that history that these films overlap with Wenders's road movies. Both mini-genres employ the same form: the first-person story of destiny. In the road movies, the protagonist arrives at his or her destiny via a journey through physical space. In these education movies, the protagonist does so via a journey across the "psychic space" separating an earlier state of mind from a later one that is manifestly and significantly different.

As in a road movie, the protagonists in these films of education start out from a state of aversion, flight, lost-ness, and fear. In this condition, the very meaning of their lives as a whole is in doubt. The cases of Finn, Sebastião, and Tomas stress that what raises the existential question is some encounter with death; in Marion's, it is the omen of the full moon. They all suggest that whenever someone is gripped by a concern for one's entire life rather than some piece of it, a figure of mortality is at its center.

Again like the road movies, in the middle of this journey of flight, the protagonist falls into a conversational entanglement with another. Thus Finn meets Flavia, and Tomas, Kate and Christopher. Damiel never exactly speaks with Marion, but his gestures at their meeting express his commitment to her idea of a communally necessary life. And in Sebastião's case, after his witnessing of human suffering and cruelty has thrown him into an inner wasteland, it is his photographic dialogue with nature's endlessly passing life that reorients him. As with the other protagonists, he is moved to affirm this conversation as one with family.

Moreover, it is striking that most of the protagonists are especially responsive to the appearing of the world. Damiel marvels at the forms of things; Finn and Sebastião are, of course, photographers. Tomas, while a writer, is shown at crucial moments, as when he is in Kate's house or in his at the end, being likewise touched by the suchness of specific objects. I believe that this kind of visual sensitivity they share is neither a coincidence nor due simply to an interest in autobiographical expression on Wenders's part. It is, rather, rooted in a vision of how we may all awaken to the sense of being at home. The features of a particular place and of the things in it that appear to one may be noticed and received affectionately. One may come to see more acutely what one cares for and one may share this insight with one's family. For affirming such a vision, the medium of cinema is virtually tailor-made.

The protagonists express their affirmations of family and home by relating their stories of destiny. Sebastião is the most explicit such narrator. Finn's narration is more intermittent and woven into the story that the film as a whole tells; the rhetorical effect is that this tale is implicitly identified as his. Most of *Wings* is a prelude to Damiel and Marion's story; her evocation of destiny at their meeting and the tutelary role that Homer plays, however, suggest that the couple's life forward will take a storytelling form. Finally, it must be acknowledged that Tomas does not at all engage in voiceover narration. Nonetheless, the fact that he is a writer and has woven his experience into his books all but identifies the film's story as his work.

The central overlap between these education movies and Wenders's road movies, then, leads me to a concluding thesis. It is that the road movies may be fairly considered a subset of his films of education. All of them in both categories portray someone's experience of being led out. In the education movies, it is as if Wenders realized that the journey from being lost to being found, from wandering to destiny, is journey enough. He can cut out the road as a superfluous middleman, particularly because the road journeys he portrays are these journeys as well. Whether or not a protagonist moves in the course of the film to a different physical place, he is manifestly changed by his inner trip into a different person. This change is fundamentally irreversible. By affirming this mortal transformation in dramatically diverse fashions —and thus letting go of the stereotypical dream of endless youth—by living a given life in various ways, the protagonists of both the road and the education movies model what it would mean for each of us to realize our own individual destinies.

Is this a realization that any of us would want to live without? In the next chapter, I examine how the understanding of education that governs our schools and sets parameters for our cultural discourse neglects, and even works against, the defining concerns of these films. Beyond simply noting that education means for Wenders something else, and leaving that as a mere curiosity or feat of art, I want to spell out what is at stake for our lives in this divergent meaning he broaches for the term. Suppose that after watching and thinking about these films, we applauded politely and then went back to taking education to be, above all, and virtually exclusively, about the acquisition of knowledge. Why would this be a problem?

5

Learning without Education

Even after I have explained how a set of Wenders's films invites us to imagine ourselves in stories of education, I have to acknowledge that some of us may remain puzzled by this invitation. We may find it hard to recognize these stories as properly educational. After all, there is a striking mismatch between the conception of education informing them and the more familiar one governing, and taught by, our schools. Far from representing a mistake, though, I want to suggest that this distinction sheds light on how our experiences of schooling can be unfulfilling. It helps us comprehend why even if one is a successful student whose work has been amply rewarded, one may feel that one's learning has left one lost. Wenders shows that this is not necessarily due to some individual pathology. It may be rooted in the fact that a person's learning can actually thwart his or her education. Hence Wenders's road and education movies are significant not only for the ways they have expanded the range of cinematic beauty and meaningfulness, but also because they draw attention to what conflating education with learning, *ēdūcere* with *ēdūcāre*, puts at risk for our lives.

How is learning, particularly as it is practiced today, likely to block education? And why is this necessarily a bad thing? These are the chief questions that guide my discussion in this chapter. Responding to them will hopefully enable me to interest not only film lovers and scholars, but also all of us who care about what schools are doing to and for us, in the works of education of Wenders and others. In order to break out of the trap of learning without education, and the way it tends to fragment and cast adrift our lives, we need to acknowledge the existence of education without learning. A good way to cultivate such an acknowledgment is to devote some of our learning practices to the study of works that imaginatively dramatize a person's realization of his or her destiny.

* * *

Learning can conflict with education only if the two things are clearly distinct. What differentiates them? As I have been explicating over the course of the book, Wenders portrays education as a story in which the protagonist realizes that his or her past life has been led by something or someone to a conversational family and an appearing home that calls for his or her devotion for the foreseeable future. At the heart of this education is a transformation of the person brought on by the revelation and affirmation that one's life has the form of a mortal, meaningful destiny. In contrast, I understand learning—and I trust I am not idiosyncratic in this—to be focused on the acquisition of knowledge. Unlike education's stress on the movement and direction of a person's life, one's path, learning emphasizes that person's accumulation and possession of things of a certain sort, one's store. The two processes are thus quite separate in kind.

Why would one want to stockpile, specifically, knowledge? Obviously, there can be any number of concrete reasons, depending on the people and the circumstances. Perhaps, though, following Hans Blumenberg, I can venture a heuristic generalization.[1] This philosopher points out that in the medieval West, we were supposed to treat curiosity as a vice that should be reined in. A hunger for knowledge could absorb one in the incidentals of the natural world and divert one away from the only essential matter: one's submission to God. The transition to modernity, then, involved the unshackling and celebration of curiosity as a virtue. Our human desire to know about all sorts of things, like many of our other desires, was no longer necessarily in conflict with a God that was now understood to be far more distant and disengaged from us and the world. Indeed, as we grew to appreciate that for the most part we have to fend for ourselves in this strange land into which we are thrown, we more urgently sought knowledge not only to gratify our curiosity but also to make this abode more secure and comfortable for our curious selves. In addition to its intrinsic value, knowledge became predominantly prized for the power it strengthens in us to predict and control objects in our lives. However many different kinds of knowledge may be available to us, from that about the latest collision of neutron stars to that about the latest celebrity marriage, the most valuable is that which makes such a pragmatic, technological difference.

---

[1] See Hans Blumenberg, *The Legitimacy of the Modern Age*, trans. Robert M. Wallace (Cambridge: MIT Press, 1983), 227–453.

Accordingly, we seek knowledge not only for the momentary pleasure it gives us in satisfying our curiosity, but also, and more importantly, because we may develop it into the means to reinforce and improve the overall quality of our lives. Guided by verifiably true beliefs about the world, we can fashion reliable instruments for domesticating it into a home ruled by our interests. As we do this, as we invest ourselves in activities of using such tools, our lives are themselves ordered into practices that are progressively more effective, efficient, and in concert with those of others. Technical knowledge thereby plays the leading role in what Max Weber dubs the rationalization of social life.[2] Indeed, by virtue of knowledgeable pedagogy, we can turn the very activity of acquiring knowledge into such a rationalized practice.

What I call learning is thus not an activity that is purely spontaneous, idiosyncratic, and occasional. It is a regular practice that exists in a field of other practices, with its own history of development and standardization. Because of this history, learning stands to some degree impersonally apart from the learner. In many instances, especially in schools, it is less strictly accurate to say "I learn x," than it is to say "I engage successfully in (generic practical exercises of) learning x." Unlike other practices, learning aims to help its central subjects, students, increase their reserve of knowledge; this is its specialty. This goal connects it to most other practices, though, since these practices depend on such knowledge for their own ongoing rationalization. Conversely, the rationalization of the entire field of social practices makes learning, too, a site of ongoing reform; researchers who study it and teachers and administrators who direct it are supposed to be constantly cooperating in order to enhance and extend its techniques.

Furthermore, the stress on technique in learning and its related practices tends to promote their growing specialization and commodification. The more a practice addresses a sharply defined part of the world, the better able it is to exercise expert mastery over that part. At the same time, as Émile Durkheim argued, the more a society divides its labor into specialized tasks, the more practitioners it can support without destructive rivalry.[3] Applying this logic to learning, then, requires the analysis and organization of the practice

---

[2] See Max Weber, *The Protestant Ethic and the Spirit of Capitalism*, trans. Talcott Parsons, ed. Richard Swedberg (New York: W. W. Norton, 2009), 3–13.
[3] See Émile Durkheim, *The Division of Labor in Society*, trans. W. D. Halls (New York: Free Press, 1984), 200–25.

into increasingly differentiated and concentrated subspecialties such as biochemical engineering education, distance education, and prekindergarten education, all geared to making certain kinds of knowledge more accessible in certain ways to certain kinds of people. New courses and degree programs are always proliferating for a wider range of narrower occupations. It can therefore be hardly surprising that such an increasingly complex, comprehensive, institutionalized, and global umbrella-practice like learning, impacting a correspondingly expanding list of other practices, demands more and more resources and amounts to a crucial investment. In the name of learning, big money is always changing hands and the bottom line can be, for many, decisive.

Although hardly thick, I trust this summary description of the specialization and commodification of the practice of learning is uncontroversial enough. In order to spell out how such learning clashes with Wendersian education, I turn to its relation to life.

* * *

"Lifelong learning." Few slogans are as familiar as this one to those of us who have sat through public celebrations at schools and colleges. At a graduation ceremony, for example, some speaker is bound to proclaim his or her belief in the idea. It is only a slight exaggeration to say that we are apt to be more surprised by the omission of such a declaration than by its recitation once again.

What does "lifelong learning" mean? The answer lies as much in the phrase's tone as in its content. It usually has a hortatory edge; it not only broadcasts what, presumably, we all count on and what the institution stands for, but also summons each of us to put that faith into practice. In effect, it is telling us to keep on learning, indefinitely.

Now since most exhortations push an audience to act in a way that to some degree it resists, it is a bit odd that this one's content is so truistic. Nobody in the world is objecting to lifelong learning. No one is contending that there is only childhood learning; no one is trying to pile up evidence to clinch the issue. It is not clear, then, why we need to be told to keep at it. Imagine how we would react if our physicians incessantly urged us to believe in lifelong breathing.

But even if we unanimously agree that lifelong learning is a good thing, we are bound to encounter serious obstacles in our efforts to walk the walk. Chief among these is the very nature of learning itself: namely, that every instance of it has a beginning and is all about coming to an end. Returning to our definition of it, learning is the activity through which someone acquires a piece of propositional knowledge or practical know-how. In certain cases, this activity is aided by a teacher; in others, not. Either way, at some point, in principle, it must be possible for the learner to realize that the acquisition process is over and he or she now knows this specific thing. Retrospectively, one should be able to say that one's learning in this instance can be traced back to a moment of origin when one first responded to a need for this particular knowledge. Now of course, I do not deny it makes sense for someone to claim on occasion that one is still learning something one does not yet have full knowledge of, as I would say that I am still learning French. My point is just that it would vitiate the very concept if we never experienced our learning bearing fruit. Built into the meaning of learning is confidence that it is generally possible. If we believe, then, that every learning activity is normally supposed to come to an end, why should we believe that we will always want to start another? Suppose I am content to live by the light of the knowledge I already have. Is that so problematic?

What gives meaning to the exhortation is the real possibility that we may each reach a point someday when we no longer feel like learning anything. "Lifelong learning" thus refers to something that at such moments we *ought to* desire. What is the basis for this prescriptive claim? Even if one is not familiar with the many treatises on this question, their answers have become common sense. Most of us take it as obvious that activities of learning, beyond bringing us knowledge, cultivate in our lives certain intellectual virtues like open-mindedness, adventurousness, seeing things from others' points of view, a problem-solving intelligence, a love of social diversity, and so on, virtues that help us individually and collectively cope with the changing world. Continuously engaging in such activities resembles continuing a regime of exercise in order to enhance and maintain the quality of our lives. When we turn our attention from what feels comfortable in the moment to our ongoing health, we are apt to realize that we do desire mental as well as physical fitness. The reason we regularly whip ourselves to keep learning, then, is that life always has to struggle against entropy—that is what it means to be alive.

The slogan "lifelong learning," in sum, affirms a link between learning activities and general quality of life. It does this in the teeth of our tendency toward death-like inertia and degradation.

Once we understand the phrase in this way, however, we find ourselves in a position to raise a critically reflective question: Do our learning activities *really* improve the quality of our lives? To be sure, legions of researchers have been empirically testing every angle of this issue. But I want to pose the question with a somewhat different stress: Do our learning activities really improve the quality of our *whole* lives? When we add the seemingly redundant adjective "whole" to the formulation, the issue becomes pointed in a more conceptual way. As I explained, because our learning activities are parts of our lives that have been largely standardized into practices tied to particular pieces of knowledge that advance particular correlated practices and foster particular qualities of character, and because we can easily observe that learning practices, like most of the practices in which we participate, are becoming more specialized every day, it is far from obvious how they *could* enhance each of our lives as a whole. To the contrary, it is at least understandable to suspect they are inviting us, teaching us, to view each of our lives as merely a shapeless bag of various qualities and abilities, like a runner's body or a knack for logic. Some of the latter may exist in historical or functional relations with each other, but perceiving these relations does not necessarily enable a person to give coherent shape to his or her life, or find a direction that is his or her own.

This becomes clearer when we view practices of learning as examples of what Georg Lukács, building on Weber, calls the reification of life.[4] Lukács develops the concept of reification as an extension of Marx's critique of commodity fetishism. The latter refers to a mode of behavior in which people mystifyingly treat social relations as relations between things.[5] For example, I, the computer I am working on at the moment, and this text may all be taken for things that stand in relation to each other and still other things according to their monetary or exchange value. Accordingly, the amount it takes to keep me alive, and to enable me to own a computer, is much greater than that which this text is likely to fetch in stores. As a consequence, my dean, representing the university that feeds me, has the authority to demand that I work on other

---

[4] See Georg Lukács, "Reification and the Consciousness of the Proletariat," in *History and Class Consciousness: Studies in Marxist Dialectics*, trans. Rodney Livingstone (Cambridge: The MIT Press, 1971), 83–222.

[5] See Karl Marx, *Capital: Volume One*, trans. Ben Fowkes (New York: Vintage Books, 1977), 163–77. Lukács acknowledges that his concept is indebted to Marx's critique in "Reification and the Consciousness of the Proletariat," 84.

tasks besides writing. The nature of our relationship is determined by the price assigned to each of us by the general market of things. Because this is a more-than-familiar scenario, the key question Marx's concept raises concerns what is particularly distorting and unnatural about this way of understanding social relations. The answer is that when we deal with people, like things, as commodities, we fail to see those people and things as *manifestations* of many-handed labor that calls for democratic organization; the tie between them and the activity that produces and maintains them is broken. Obscured is the fact that my dean and I, as well as our university and the computers and texts in it, all testify to a prior and invaluable network of human creativity that is essentially cooperative. Marx's critique asks us to acknowledge this reality and work out its implications for how our society is governed and its resources distributed. He wants to enhance expressly the unrecognized cooperation we are already relying on.

Now Lukács examines how this mystifying form of behavior has expanded in our societies to affect not only the realm of production but also every dimension of human life.

> [Commodity fetishism] stamps its imprint upon the whole consciousness of man; his qualities and abilities are no longer an organic part of his personality, they are things which he can "own" or "dispose of" like the various objects of the external world. And there is no natural form in which human relations can be cast, no way in which man can bring his physical and psychic "qualities" into play without their being subjected increasingly to this reifying process. We need only think of marriage, and . . . the way in which [Immanuel] Kant, for example, described the situation with the naively cynical frankness peculiar to great thinkers. "Sexual community," he says, "is the reciprocal use made by one person of the sexual organs and faculties of another . . . marriage is the union of two people of different sexes with a view to the mutual possession of each other's sexual attributes for the duration of their lives."[6]

No wonder poor Immanuel never wed. At any event, Lukács elucidates how our individual and communal lives are being increasingly broken down into compartmentalized parts that we can own, buy, and sell. What prepares us for this reification is our subjection to the process of Weberian rationalization I

---

[6] Lukács, "Reification and the Consciousness of the Proletariat," 100.

described earlier, particularly to specialized, ostensibly scientific, causal laws for prediction and control that place elements of a person's life in systematic relation both to each other, and, not incidentally, to a market that supports them, and cut off such a part or practice from the totality of life. Sex is, indeed, an illuminating example. Instead of being understood to be something like a quality of people's lives as a whole, it is commonly treated as a specific, gothic drive that can be mastered by knowing technicians equipped with the tools of the trade. Beyond pleasure seeking, such people may learn to use sex to sell things and wield influence. As a condition for this sort of manipulation to occur, though, the drive must be reducible to calculable, quantitative measures so that its experiences and props may be assigned their proper cash value. No one should be surprised, then, when someone figures out that these experiences are not worth lifelong financial support—particularly when one turns to consider other, separate practices in which one is invested.

As this book's opening fable suggests, many of us would be revolted if all of our sexual experiences and actions were as a rule to be understood in these reifying, alienating terms. Yet, similar calculations are at work in the practice of learning. A learner is supposed to be a customer and a commodity. Skills, experience, expertise: these are all taken to be resources in one's life that one can own and sell, like things with more overt price tags such as course points and job qualifications. What one is supposed to be searching to buy is a desirable career or "living"—the ultimate reification of life. Accordingly, the reason one may be willing to shell out significant time, effort, and money for, say, a college degree is that one reckons the living the degree is likely to enable one to earn is worth the cost compared to the living one would probably have to accept without the degree. This is why we commonly celebrate learning in terms of the capabilities and range of choices it fosters.

Empowerment and freedom are, of course, good things. Lukács's critical point, however, is that such a reified practice of learning, understood to serve and promote the reification of other practices, pressures us to think of our very selves as a collection of parts that we invest in and make tradeoffs among. A default direction for pursuing these deals is determined by the haphazardly fluctuating market value of these commodities. If we do not understand ourselves in this way, we will be imprudently setting ourselves up to be losers. For this reason, our gurus are often career counselors. Now such an understanding suits a society composed of workers competing to prove their efficiency, and of consumers seeking the most effective ways to get what they want. But it leaves unaddressed—not to mention discounts as foolishly impractical—questions of how these parts belong to and form an "organic" self, and of how they harmonize with the "natural form in which human relations can be cast." Utterly concealed is the sense, dramatized in Wenders's films, that prior to being a worker or consumer (or someone who profits from them), I am a mortal longing to live a meaningful life, receptive to the guidance of equally mortal, human company.

A glance at the work of Donald Judd, a prominent minimalist sculptor, may also illustrate this concern. Although he started out as an easel painter, Judd soon rejected the traditional painting because he saw it as a "vague whole" consisting of "definite parts" in some kind of intricate order. What he wanted to pursue, instead, were works that project the sense of a "definite *whole* and maybe no parts, or very few." As he grasped it, "the big problem is to maintain the sense of the whole thing."[7] Analogously, no matter how many items we have learned and continue to learn, we may feel that none of them or even their sum enables us to address the big problem: How do we not only determine and perform the right actions appropriate to a particular set of momentary circumstances, but also live meaningfully a whole life?

In the light of this reasonable anxiety that anyone may experience, the uncanniness of lifelong learning may now be more striking. On the one hand, the prospect of being caught up for a lifetime in acquiring discrete pieces of knowledge for increasing one's mastery of correspondingly specialized practices may be precisely what arouses and fuels skepticism that such learning, or perhaps anything else, could ever help one comprehend one's singular life. "Lifelong learning," in this sense, would be a dispiriting phrase, alluding to something that it stifles and supplants. On the other hand, precisely by virtue of this allusion, this phrase could evoke the possible existence of some special, alternative kind of learning experience that begins at birth and stretches to the day we die. Perhaps this other learning could focus on an equally exceptional kind of knowledge, call it wisdom, that discloses an entire life's meaning. Taking thought of this strange doublesidedness, then, we may translate "lifelong learning" into "learning for life," which displays

---

[7] All of these quotes of Judd's come from Bruce Glaser, "Questions to Stella and Judd," in *Minimal Art: A Critical Anthology*, ed. Gregory Battock (New York: E. P. Dutton, 1968), 154.

more explicitly two opposed meanings: learning one damn thing after another for the indefinite future, and learning as a way of living a whole life. An ambiguous and contradictory phrase that can express both resignation and hope—it appears we are no longer talking about a mere platitude to pad out a graduation speech.

This suggests that lifelong learning is a symptom of a kind of cultural neurosis. Proclaiming belief in it so regularly and ritualistically enables members of our culture to express and even celebrate a longing to learn how one should live a coherent life. But because the meaning that is actually enforced by our institutional customs is that we should keep on learning more specialties, the phrase in effect denies the validity or even existence of this longing. Such a symbolic expression of a desire, combined with its practical repression, indicates that we are disowning a dimension of ourselves integral to our lives, while settling for a fantasy of what we want. Weber's portrait of the result can hardly be bettered: "specialists without spirit, sensualists without heart."[8]

Much more needs to be elucidated about why we repress this desire to learn how we should live a life, and what else, besides our acceptance of this dimension of ourselves, this repression is costing us. But for the purposes of this project, I want to stay modestly focused on the relation of learning to education. Out of my previous discussion of Wenders's road and education movies, I would like now to derive a concept of education as destiny that addresses less inhibitedly and more constructively our longing. Conversely, this concept directs us to look for guidance in living a life less in practices inside or even outside the classroom, than in a type of work of artistic culture like these of Wenders.

* * *

"Education as destiny": how does the meaning of this phrase, which I am going to theorize, diverge from that of "lifelong learning"? I propose that we employ the former phrase to affirm that one is trying to live in a coherent way a whole life; it means this affirmation. It thus echoes the existentially hopeful interpretation, so to speak, of lifelong learning. This resonance conforms to our conventional expectation that education and learning are closely related.

---

[8] Weber, *The Protestant Ethic*, 96.

However, I want to break from the notion that they are synonymous by claiming that education affirms one is living a whole life non-contradictorily; it can do this precisely because it is no longer reducible to learning. Accordingly, education initially means *not* the normal getting of knowledge, especially when our concern is restricted to the success and failure of this acquisition. This negation registers the understanding that one's learning practices tend to treat as nothing precisely what one's education means to affirm. Once more, I am not at all denying that there are plenty of reasons to treasure and pursue learning; I have already discussed some principal ones. I am merely noting that by my proposed definition, an education expresses an interest that is usually absent in such learning.

How it does this is an equally crucial part of its meaning. The words "my education" that come out of my mouth flow from the felt sweep of an entire life. Their utterance is backed by that kind of momentum and hence has a lyric quality. To register this, I postulate that my education, my affirming my life, *is* my living that life, as distinct from acting to master a moment in it. Hence when we unpack the phrase in a bit more detail, we arrive not at "my education about life," or "my education for quality of life," but, rather, "my education *as* my life."

Part of what makes this formulation still obscure, however, is the term *life*, which has many different associations. Let me try to consolidate some of the main ones. For instance, *life* can connote the energy that animates us, on the one hand, yet which ebbs and flows, on the other. Since we are specifically interested in the quality of wholeness that lifelong learning contradictorily affirms, perhaps we can fold this vitalist understanding of life into one that is focused less on momentary fluctuations and more on continuity across time marked by change.

Such a focus is reminiscent of the concept of formation. Is this the understanding of life we are looking for? Formation happens over a period of time; it is caused by events that change us; these changes lead us to understand that our lives have a particular past and direction. John Dewey would add that formation manifests our ongoing growth.[9] It thus stresses our historical dimension. But does this dimension necessarily pertain to an entire life?

---

[9] See John Dewey, "Education as Growth," in *Democracy and Education: An Introduction to the Philosophy of Education* (New York: The Free Press, 1944), 41–53.

For every Goethe composing a novel about *Bildung*, there is a job applicant composing a resume of his *formation professionelle*. In order to stipulate that formation concerns the whole of a person's life, we need to reach for a supplementary concept.

Hence I turn to that of fate. My fate places my life in the shadow of my death and thereby acknowledges a limit that unifies it. A whole life is a mortal one. As mine takes place over time, it is marked by certain experiences and actions, on the one hand, and not others that I had no time for, on the other. The actual moments form my life history that is meaningfully distinct from the alternative possible histories my death leaves unrealized. Moreover, in the visions of fatal formation articulated in ancient Greek theater and American film noir, as we briefly reviewed in Chapter 4, what lead me to this history's completion are shadowy forces that do not so much kill me as ironically twist my intentions. I become the unwitting puppet of the gods or a femme fatale; such figures personify the way my actions to defer death may be exactly what hasten it. The history of my fate is thus one of blind self-destruction. No wonder, as Aristotle remarked, contemplation of it arouses pity and fear.[10]

The *Poetics* tells us, furthermore, where we should look if we want to understand our fateful struggles. These do not belong to a set list of battlefields. There are no fate-forming practices in particular for us to engage in and reform. Nonetheless, the struggles can be, and have been, captured in literary and artistic works that did not fall from the sky labeled "tragedy," but were assembled under that name by discerning audiences. When we join Aristotle and a tradition of others in studying these works, we take part in a constitutive conversation on the nature and significance of education as fatal formation.

Suppose, then, we are motivated to equate education with fate because we appreciate that the formation of a whole life is rooted in a sense of mortality. Does it necessarily follow that this formation has to be focused on an end we all fear and strive in vain to avoid? Is this the only way of conceiving of death? The alternative I propose, again inspired by Wenders's films, is that of understanding our existence from birth as one extensive process of dying. Let formation refer not to the history of our lives, but to that of our deaths. Seeing things in this way then prompts the question of what it could mean to die over

---

[10] See Aristotle, *Poetics*, trans. I. Bywater, in *The Complete Works of Aristotle*, ed. Jonathan Barnes (Princeton: Princeton University Press, 1984).

a lifetime willingly and meaningfully. And one answer is that it would mean giving away your life to something. My active dying would be the constant sacrifice of my life to something more important than its preservation and enhancement. Works like *Alice in the Cities* or *The Salt of the Earth*, as well as Augustine's *Confessions* or George Eliot's *Middlemarch*, testify to the possibility of this kind of devotion.

We often describe such a devotional life with the term *calling*. As a revision of the concept of fatal formation, which stresses the finality of the noun, a formative calling is more explicitly open-ended. Identifying my education with it would entail my affirming and living my life not only as historical and mortal, but also for the sake of something beyond me that attracts me into the wondrous unknown. Indeed, the concept of calling also inflects the vitalist understanding of life: it suggests that as an animating energy, life does not push, but pulls us. Correspondingly, my dying need not be an experience of the loss of self-assertiveness; it can be one of inspired generosity. Admittedly, a work like *Middlemarch* or Sigmund Freud's *Civilization and Its Discontents*, or Wenders's *Land of Plenty*, alerts us to the tendency of a calling to become intoxicated with ascetic high-mindedness: flying close to the sun can be tragically blinding and destructive. But we can take these as cautionary words rather than as last ones.

Why, then, am I not theorizing education as a calling? The reason is a matter of rhetorical nuance: I worry that this concept suggests the most important feature of my life is that it is being drawn along in a certain direction from the outside, rather passively. In contrast, as I have repeatedly noted, I use the phrase "my education" to affirm my living a life. This implies that this affirmation matters and makes a crucial difference to me as such. Strictly speaking, my devotional life is less a calling than my being actively true to one.

Indeed, comparable to the way that warranted, objectively true belief or knowledge is at the center of learning, I want to suggest that a different kind of truth is key to education as destiny. Usually, we think of truth as a quality that belongs principally to beliefs or propositions. In accordance with this, it makes sense for someone to claim that the assertion that such-and-such a thing is a chair is true. By extension, we can assign truth to other objects as well, such as when we remark that something is a true chair or someone a true friend. Examples of the latter sort, though, can always be analyzed into propositional truths: when asked to explain why I believe that a particular person is a true friend, I usually have recourse to statements that claim it is true that people who act in such-and-such a fashion count as friends. And to be sure, if I am pressed to elaborate on what it means that this proposition is true, I am apt to reply that it represents how things really are in the world and not merely how they seem to be, to me or to someone else.

Departing from this objective understanding of truth, Søren Kierkegaard, who devoted himself to the somewhat paradoxical project of theorizing faith, declares his interest in "subjective truth."[11] What might this mean? I take him to be claiming that there is additionally a kind of truth that is a quality not of propositions but of lives. What is true, in this case, is how someone leads his or her life. And what makes someone's life true? It is the way that person is *true to* something or someone. Active devotion to what is more important, more meaningful, than the person's self-preservation or enhancement is its mark. In contrast, what makes an uncommitted life correspondingly false is that it pretends it has no need for meaning. Now, of course, it is possible for a critic to object that there is no compelling reason to hold this subjective understanding of truth to be objectively true to the real nature of human beings. Maybe it is possible for the species to live without meaning. If one reflects on one's own very real, individual mortality, however, it may become clear what is concretely at stake in the possibility of making a subjective decision, a Pascalian wager.[12] A true life may promise to me immeasurably more than does an uncommitted one. I may thus decide to be true to a person as his or her friend. In this spirit, my devotion to a calling is not based on something I know, some set of beliefs I have that force me to acknowledge their necessary and objective truth. It grows out of a commitment to believe in something definite that is possible, risky, and inviting. Something to freely love.

But what if such a leap of faith serves as a prelude to murder? Should we not discourage such fanaticism by denying that sheer devotion could have anything to do with truth? History is, of course, full of bloody examples of the danger here. My reply is to note that it is also full of events that testify to the impotence of appeals to objective, absolutely necessary, quasi-mathematical truths and laws in preventing cruelty and violence. I doubt there are any forms

---

[11] See Søren Kierkegaard, *Concluding Unscientific Postscript to Philosophical Fragments*, ed. and trans. Howard V. Hong and Edna H. Hong (Princeton: Princeton University Press, 1992).

[12] See Blaise Pascal, *Pensées*, ed. and trans. Roger Ariew (Indianapolis: Hackett: 2005), 212–14.

of persuasion that are guaranteed to disarm us. By recognizing that a person's orientation to the world and others is ultimately a matter of faith, though, we may remind him or her that it is not based on certainty. Because one does not know the nature of what is calling one, one is also bound to admit that what it is calling one to do is irreducibly mysterious, unclear, and open to question. Humility is called for. This check on self-righteousness, I believe, can be an opening for pacifying conversation.

A related issue concerns the possibility of trueness to something, fidelity, devolving into wishful thinking. Consider the example of a Christian boy who believes that his repeated attractions to other boys are a lure of the Devil. Suppose that an atheist friend points out that he seems to be using his faith as a way to flee accepting responsibility for his authentic homosexuality. Should the latter, plausible description of the situation override the boy's declarations of his subjective truth? Should the friend insist that the boy's beliefs bow before objective reality, on pain of representing a self-delusive lie? The reason I think not is that someone's subjective truth can never in principle be closed to revision as such. In this particular case, nothing prevents the boy, in response to friendly advice, from modifying his understanding of his Christian faith, or placing his faith in a non-Christian understanding of his life and world that does a better job of making sense of his sexuality—without abandoning the central drama of being true to something. If he were ever to come to treat the latter as mere idle fancy, it would be because he has forgotten what is mortally at stake in it.

Education as destiny, then, is meant to complete the sense of being called with the understanding that what is formative is one's being true to that calling. One's calling may be defined more narrowly as an encounter with grace. In response, one affirms one's whole, mortal, historical life led up to this moment; one tries to integrate all the events and features of one's past, including those that at first traumatically overloaded one, into a story of how this encounter took place. Furthermore, this history, in turn, forms a path for one to follow through on and live forward. My destiny is accordingly the speech-act of telling the story of my life, to others or myself, as one about a journey to and from grace. It is my answer to Zarathustra's question about what makes fate loveable: "Have you ever said Yes to a single joy?"[13] For Nietzsche and me, this question

---

[13] Nietzsche, *Thus Spoke Zarathustra*, 323.

can be meaningful only because my destiny is precisely *not* predestined or given in advance. I have to claim it by demonstrating my love of fate, that is, by authoring and committing my life to this kind of story; this is what it means to wholeheartedly say yes to anything. When I equate this storytelling with my education, then, I express my belief that it affirms more consistently the hope in lifelong learning. And that it spells out more clearly the realization that my life is an education.

What brings me to such an act of storytelling? On the one hand, of course, it is certain kinds of experiences I have had, especially those of being lost, of being found, and of understanding the turning between the two as an event of grace that calls me to say yes with my life. Outside of them, nothing can force me to recognize my life as an education.

Even these experiences would not constitute one, however, unless I have not also become conversant with stories in general and education stories in particular. One needs to develop an understanding, on the other hand, of the education story form and of how it may accommodate and make sense of one's various and unique experiences, orienting them to the four questions of being led out. The most likely way for this to take place is if a corpus of exemplary works of education is widely available and celebrated. Although a person's inner experiences are to a significant degree bound to be idiosyncratic, we as a society can do something to champion these external works publicly. Education as destiny is thus also an appreciative name for their genre. It designates how Wenders's road and education movies, for instance, are part of an even larger family of works that culturally supports our individual educations.

To nourish this genre, akin to the way we do this for that of tragedy, we should seek to draw serious attention to works in the various arts, such as novels, songs, paintings, and dances, which flesh out recognizable details of a person's education. Our aim should be to place a growing list of such works in conversation with each other and with the conventions that they share and play off. This entails elaborating comparative judgments about them that will hopefully stimulate insightful argument and discussion among an audience that extends beyond their authors. Moreover, because many of the works have already been the object of critical examination, we should try to explain how our educational readings address lingering problems or lacunae in their interpretation. By thus claiming, one case at a time, that certain works are useful for understanding education as destiny, and that education as destiny is useful for understanding certain works, we substantiate the genre's existence.

This project of scholarship should be complemented by one of teaching, one of drawing more and more people in different walks of life into conversation with such representations of destiny. We thereby make it easier for all of us to imagine that our lives, too, may be an education. Needless to say, we will need to acquire knowledge about a lot of things in order to engage with this genre of works. The cultivation of education as destiny calls us to pursue and support various practices of learning, particularly those that develop one's literacy. In the end, then, education as *ēdūcere* does need to be wed to education as *ēducāre*. Even as we recognize more clearly the difference between these terms, and the ways they may pull us in conflicting directions, we should affirm that they ultimately belong together.

Wenders's road and education movies can both spur and contribute to these cultural projects. An apt closing title card for these films, I have been arguing, is not "the end," or even "to be continued," but Rilke's "you must change your life."[14] Suppose we do not, however. Suppose that we continue to leave undeveloped and near invisible the multifarious yet collective stress of this genre of artworks on education as destiny. Instead of articulating with their help the possibility of each of us being led out on a meaningful life path, suppose we go along with the reproduction of the realm of learning without education. It teaches us that a person's life is a chance miscellany of practical possibilities and limitations, and that living is a matter of making out of this the most prudent deals for pleasurable things on a moment-to-moment basis. Indeed, it insists, it is impossible that there be an alternative to this realm more responsive to education—*education* and *learning* are merely different words for the same thing. If we thus accept this, and return to this book's opening fable, on what rational grounds, then, could we object to the loveless prostitutes from another planet? How alien would they be really?

---

[14] "Du mußt dein Leben ändern." See Rainer Maria Rilke, "Archaic Torso of Apollo," in *Ahead of All Parting: The Selected Poetry and Prose of Rainer Maria Rilke*, ed. and trans. Stephen Mitchell (New York: The Modern Library, 1995), 66–7.

6

Coda

Dear Kert,

You're probably shocked to see me addressing you in such a familiar way, rather than as "Senator 3, Congress 5." I swear it's not out of disrespect; I need to appeal to that inseparable friend who knew me when I was just starting out. I'm still that person who has no interest in playing games, Kert, the same one you trusted to listen when you had second thoughts about that student government post. Your old confidante is calling for your serious attentiveness today because I have an urgent request, one that is actually quite humiliating for me, and one which may be fully comprehensible only if it is viewed in relation to our youth. In the name of what we lived through together, please consider with care what I'm about to ask of you before you say no!

After such a lunging flourish, it may be best if I step back and start over with a little routine news. Everything has been getting better since we all left Earth last month. Thankfully, morale has been bouncing back, at least somewhat, not only on our ship but in the entire fleet. I suppose even trained and experienced scientists couldn't possibly have been prepared for that planet's travesty of education. Alien worlds are one thing, but a positively infernal one, one that pretends to celebrate the very thing it perverts? I know the media can't get enough of the outrageousness of it all; the story they've been missing, though, is how this encounter has broken the spirits of even some of our most adventurous explorers. The captain who was the most eager to participate in the original expedition years ago, the one who played such a pivotal role in the first contact—you know who I'm talking about even though names aren't allowed—has become obsessed now with the possibility that her mind has been corrupted. I tell you, when this news of how many of us have been crippled starts to leak out, it may be curtains for the entire space program.

Of course, a little while ago, I wouldn't exactly have mourned that. I can see your eyes widening: no, I haven't forgotten my part in recent events and I don't mean to downplay it. Every word of that report on Earth's learning system and its effects I sent you, Senator 3, Congress 5, remains verifiably accurate. And I still feel honored that my recommendations spurred you to such stirring and principled action. The campaign for Earth divestment is fortunate, indeed, to have a leader like you.

So you're right, after uncovering the planet's horrific situation, I was transparently all for an indefinite ban on further interstellar research. Speaking more personally, I still haven't found a way to drive out of my mind the images of resigned and cynical, lost Earth youths cramming in libraries for their college entrance exams, all in the name of "education." Every single face in those armies I observed appeared just as engulfed in darkness as the stars outside my window. It was not only frightening, but also devastating. My relief knew no bounds, then, when we all heard of your triumph. No one was more grateful at being rescued than I; no one longed more for their family. The whole notion of leaving home seemed like an incomprehensible mistake.

You may be wondering, though, why I'm describing these sentiments in the past tense. Has something changed? Does it have to do with why, in the middle of this journey between worlds, I am writing to you?

This is where our personal past comes in, Kert. Remember: the same year you pulled off that upset in your first election, I realized I was called to be an extraterrestrial anthropologist of education. We gave each other such crucial support during those difficult, first baby steps toward something to love—all those all-night talks, and that one day of tears. Your friendship meant the world to me and I can never think of it without being deeply moved. I trust you recall, then, that as I struggled to commit myself to a path, my primary passion was for education. It was because the idea that our lives take the form of destinies so filled my imagination and so fired me up, that I couldn't wait to discover how such destinies look and are celebrated in foreign cultures. And naturally, it's because of this passion that I could barely maintain the anthropologist's composure when I got to Earth.

You would think, then, that as I flee the barbarians and return into the embrace of civilization, there can be no room for ambivalence. But this is what has gradually and surprisingly dawned on me. As much as I cherish our culture, I have to acknowledge there's something stale about it. The yearly round of holidays and awards for select works and projects has become something we all nod along with, thoughtlessly. We take for granted our support of education; we treat reminders of it impatiently as so many needless platitudes. Hence the insight I came to, and which is penetrating me at present, is that what led me out was actually not only love of education; it was anguish that so many fellow, professed lovers of it appear to have lost their appreciation of what it truly means. I know this sounds crazy: how can a culture that ubiquitously reminds us about an idea cause us to forget it? I can hardly understand this myself. Nevertheless, as I approach our home world, I'm becoming surer about what I'm feeling. A beautiful line from one of the Earth philosophers, Søren Kierkegaard, expresses its pith: in all of Christendom, where is there a Christian? My very run-in with an uneducated planet of learners has strangely awakened in me an analogous worry about our educationdom, and about the authenticity of my own calling.

Yes, I'm slipping back into our youthful, grandiose mode of talk, but please, in memory of what that conversation meant to us both, hear me out. As I struggle with my mounting and perplexing ambivalence on this voyage, two additional conversations into which I had entered on Earth are beginning to give it focus. The first is with a college professor who was part of my fourth study. By that time, I could barely stand to be around "teachers"—before you berate me for my language, remember this is what they call themselves—but this guy was different from the ones I had up to then interviewed. Although he was entirely average in talent and achievement, he agonized over his limited ability to help his students live meaningful lives. Even when he made this aim the explicit theme of his courses, featuring it in class discussions and in reading and writing assignments, he again and again ran up against the fact that the students were already trained by the learning system's structural features to contain reductively the theme's seriousness, to repress it. How could thinking about their lives be for them anything more than a prerequisite for a good grade? The two of us ended up spending a fair amount of time together as I worked to get a clearer understanding of his discontent. Eventually, I discovered that if you had eyes for it, that frustration was in quite a number of other teachers, too. As you know, I wove some of their accounts into my report. What I didn't suspect at the time, however, is that finding a piece of myself in teachers like him could transform how I view Earth. Instead of an anti-educational culture, I'm now starting to see a pre-educational one. I'm wondering if teachers, people who are charged with the task of repressing education among the young, yet people who are also struggling with their own uneducated commitment to this task, may be in a key, frontline position to act as agents of change.

At around the same time, one evening, after I had finished shadowing him for the day, this professor invited me to a screening of a film, *Alice in the Cities*. It was part of a New York retrospective on the cinematic work of Wim Wenders called *Portraits along the Road*. The film enthralled me and I made it a point to see the remaining works in that series (which wasn't easy because almost every showing was sold out) and to hunt down video copies of Wenders's oeuvre. As you would expect, the films tell stories about a variety of characters in different situations. What intrigues me, what *delights* me, though, is the road many of them share: it is precisely that of education as destiny! As in so many works in Earth culture, there's not a word about what *we* call education—yet there it is, arousing popular appreciation to boot! And what profoundly moves and impresses me, old friend, is that these films portray the travelers realizing their education only through intense struggle. They bring home to us what a vital achievement one's education can feel like.

As I have dwelled on, and pursued internally, my conversations with the unhappy professor and with Wenders's education movies, I've started to imagine what could happen if such teachers and films entered into conversation with each other. Suppose that filmmakers, as well as other artists and thinkers, could believe that their works help inspire and sustain a project to reform the planet's anti-educational system of learning, that these works mean something more than a few hours of entertaining distraction. And suppose that teachers, wrestling with their dissatisfaction about the status quo, with their flickering confidence that another world is possible, and with the concrete challenges and tests to their commitment to such an incremental, world-altering project, could feel less isolated and self-doubting. Would not both groups then be drawing from each other support not only for building a general culture of education, but also for affirming their own particular education? Like you and I did?

Indeed, it appears to me that there already exists an institutional place on the planet for this synergistic dialogue to take root: namely, in what the earthlings call "liberal education." These days, that institution is beleaguered by questions about its market value and is very much in danger of being either cut out altogether or repurposed into yet another vehicle of reifying learning. But what if it were to grow, instead, in distinction and influence, nourished by attention to exemplary works of education like Wenders's and to the longing for education in people like the professor? What if this part of schooling could serve education? Could this not constitute a hope for these beings who are perhaps not so very alien after all?

You see where I'm going. Believe me, it's not easy to admit that my earlier, rather forceful, counsel to you was in error. I saw only the threat that Earth posed to the culture we love. It was imperative to protect it. Now, though, I see that our culture can also wither away complacently. It may become senile, forgetting that it actually stands for something. The single most shocking thing I have to say to you, Kert, is hence this: the encounter with the aliens, I now realize, is for us grace. It presents us with the sobering opportunity to recall how a culture of education made a difference to our ancestors, and can still do so to us, by contemplating what its absence looks like. Furthermore, this encounter may not only reawaken cultural devotion; it may also give us a concrete way to express it. We may help the earthlings struggle for their own education. We may thus risk ourselves for, give ourselves to, education once again!

Now that my request is anticlimactic, then, it's easier for me to muster the temerity to make it. Senator 3, Congress 5, please consider reversing course. Please try to persuade your colleagues to throw themselves with equal passion and effectiveness into a reinvest-in-Earth campaign. You have my blessing to publicly blame the previous wrong move on me. Hear my seriousness, Kert: I'm ready to be stripped of my position and reputation and to live with the deprivation. All I want, all I have ever wanted, is to serve meaningfully the home idea we all serve. Remember?

Yours truly,
Rats

Index

Adventures of Huckleberry Finn, The 7
Alabama (short film) 19 n.1
Alice in the Cities (film) 8, 15, 16, 17, 19–22, 78, 143, 152
   aesthetics and importance in 31
   destiny in 37–9
   episodic form in 34–5
   familial feelings in 36–7
   images and importance in 22–5, 32, 33
   motivation and significance in 28–9
   resemblance with *Kings of the Road* 43, 46
   self and self-centredness in 25–8
   sentiment and significance in 32
aloneness/loneliness 43–5, 48, 51, 52, 68, 73, 75, 95–8, 114. *See also* isolation; solitude/solitary
American Friend, The (film) 16, 72, 92–5
Antonioni, M. 111
anxiety 73, 75, 93, 115, 139
Archer, N. 79 n.1
Arisha, the Bear, and the Stone Ring (short film) 41 n.1
Aristotle 142

Badiou, A. 11
Badlands (film) 7, 79
"Ballad of Easy Rider" (song) 94
Bergman, I. 111 n.3, 112, 114
Bernhard, T. 97
Berry, C. 30
Bildungsroman (novel of formation) 8, 16, 72, 95, 99
Blow-up (film) 111
Blumenberg, H. 132
Bonnie and Clyde (film) 7, 79
Bordwell, D. 21
Buena Vista Social Club (film) 8
Buñuel, L. 96

calling, concept of 143
Canned Heat 29

Cavell, S. 12–13
Civilization and Its Discontents (Freud) 143
commodity fetishism 136–7
Conditions Handsome and Unhandsome (Cavell) 12–13
Confessions (Augustine) 143
conversation, significance of 9, 13, 36–7, 46, 47, 49, 53, 59, 61–3, 66, 69, 75–7, 96, 97, 105, 106, 112, 116, 127, 142, 145–7, 151, 152

death, portrayals of 34, 44, 54, 73, 80, 89–95, 112, 114–16, 121, 122, 126, 127, 142
destiny 15, 16–17, 20, 37–9, 41–3, 47, 59, 68–71, 74, 77, 78, 83–6, 88–90, 100, 103, 109, 110, 114, 116, 121, 127, 128, 131, 132, 140, 143, 145–7, 150, 152
   and fate compared 92, 95, 145–6
Detour (film) 16, 72, 91–2
Dewey, J. 141
dialectical thinking 9
Divine Comedy, The 7
Don't Come Knocking (film) 16, 41, 64–9, 103
   existential crisis in 65–6
   familial feelings in 69
   family resemblance in 68
   heroic individual image in 68–9
   lost in isolation in 68
   resemblance with *Paris, Texas* 68
Drifters, The 21
Durkheim, E. 133
Dylan, Bob 95

Easy Rider (film) 16, 71, 79–81
   resemblance with *Kings of the Road* 81
   resemblance with *Land of Plenty* 81
education, as calling 143–5
education, as destiny 140–7

education movies
   Every Thing Will Be Fine 121–6
   Palermo Shooting 110–16
   Salt of the Earth, The 116–21
   Wings of Desire 104–10
ēdūcere 6
   ēdūcāre and 3–4, 42, 147
Eliot, G. 143
Emersonian perfectionism 13
epic form 107
Every Thing Will Be Fine (film) 17, 121–6
   resemblance with *Palermo Shooting* 126
Exodus (photographs) 119

Falk, P. 108
family relation 14–16, 20, 32–3, 36–7, 42, 49, 50, 52, 56, 57, 62, 63, 68, 76–7, 86, 93, 101, 118, 126, 128
Faraway, So Close! (film) 110
Fatalism in American Film Noir (Pippin) 89–90
fatalism, significance of 92, 94, 123, 142, 143
fate 89–90, 92, 112, 142
   and destiny compared 92, 95, 145–6
femme fatale, significance of 90, 92, 142
Five Easy Pieces (film) 79
flight, trope of 72–3
Ford, J. 23, 34, 49
formation, concept of 141–2
formative calling 143
Freud, S. 143
Friedrich, C. D. 100
"From Her to Eternity" (song) 108

gaze 29, 52, 63, 83, 96
Genesis (photographs) 120
Glaser, B. 139 n.7
Goalie's Anxiety at the Penalty Kick (film) 19 n.1
Goethe, J. W. von 8, 98, 99

Hamm, P. 107 n.2
Handke, P. 8, 37, 95, 104, 107 n.2
Heidegger, M. 6
Herzog, W. 88
Hopper, D. 79, 94, 114

"I Just Sing" (song) 96
"I Pity the Poor Immigrant" (song) 95
isolation 63, 68, 73. See also aloneness/loneliness; solitude/solitary

Judd, D. 139

Kant, I. 137
Keough, P. 54 n.3
Kerouac, J. 26
Kierkegaard, S. 144, 151
"King of the Road" (song) 46
Kings of the Road (film) 16, 41, 43–7, 63, 81
   destiny in 47
   episodic form in 44–5
   male gaze in 45
   resemblance with *Alice in the Cities* 43, 46
Kinski, N. 53

Laderman, D. 79
Land of Plenty (film) 16, 41, 60–4, 68, 69, 76, 81, 143
   absent mother's influence in 63
   episodic form in 61
   resemblance with *Alice in the Cities* 61
lifelong learning 134–40
   as cultural neurosis 140
Lisbon Story (film) 16, 41 n.2, 71, 81–3
   destiny in 83
Lukács, G. 136, 137
Lusty Men, The (film) 45

Marx, K. 9
"Memphis, Tennessee" (song) 30
Middlemarch (Eliot) 143
Miller, R. 46

narrative cinema, significance of 25–6
Natural Born Killers (film) 7
Nick Cave and the Bad Seeds 108
Nietzsche, F. 9–11, 145

Odyssey 7
On the Road 7
"On the Road Again" (song) 29
Ordinary People (film) 76

Other Americas (photographs)   117
Ozu, Y.   36, 76, 86

Palermo Shooting (film)   17, 110–16
  death in   114–15
  destiny in   114
  resemblance with *Alice in the Cities*   113, 114
  resemblance with *Kings of the Road*   114
  resemblance with *Lisbon Story*   113
Palin, M.   85
Paris, Texas (film)   8, 16, 41, 48–54
  familial feelings in   52
  male gaze in   52
  resemblance with *Kings of the Road*   51
Pascal, B.   144 n.12
perfectionism   13
Pina (documentary)   122
Pippin, R.   89
Poetics (Aristotle)   142
postmodernization   86

Rain People, The (film)   79
rationalization, of social practice   133
Ray, N.   45
reading and thematization   14
redemption   9, 20, 31, 37, 69, 78, 82 n.3, 83, 99, 119
Redford, Robert   76
Red Wheelbarrow, The (poem)   35
reification   136–8
Return of Jesse James, The (film)   67
Rilke, R. M.   147

Sahel: The End of the Road (photographs)   118
St. Augustine   143
Salgado, J. R.   116, 117
Salgado, S.   116–20
Salt of the Earth, The   17, 116–21, 143
Seventh Seal, The (film)   114
Shepard, S.   64, 75
solitude/solitary   22, 29, 43–6, 54, 61, 73. *See also* aloneness/loneliness; isolation
State of Things, The (film)   82 n.3

subjective truth   144, 145
Submergence (film)   7
Sugarland Express, The (film)   79
Summer in the City (film)   19 n.1

3 American LPs (short film)   19 n.1
Tokyo-ga (documentary film)   16, 71, 86–9
  as anti-travelogue   86
Troggs, The   96
Twelve Miles to Trona (short film)   41 n.1
Two-Lane Blacktop (film)   79

Ulmer, E. G.   91
"Under the Boardwalk" (song)   21
Until the End of the World (film)   16, 41, 54–60, 68
  destiny in   59
  images and significance in   58–9
  resemblance with *Alice in the Cities*   55, 58, 59

valuation, approach to   10–11
Vogler, R.   43

Wanderer above the Sea of Fog (painting)   100
Weber, M.   133
Wenders, Wim   7–8, 20 n.1. *See also* individual entries
Wild at Heart (film)   7
Wilhelm Meister's Apprenticeship (Goethe)   8, 16, 72, 95, 98
Williams, W. C.   35
Wings of Desire (film)   8, 16, 104–9
  destiny in   109
  epic form in   107
  on war   108
Wittgenstein, L.   14
Workers (photographs)   118
Wrong Move (film)   16, 43, 72, 95–101
  resemblance with *Alice in the Cities*   96
  resemblance with *Wilhelm Meister's Apprenticeship*   98–9

Young Mr. Lincoln (film)   23